Prayer Is Not an Option It's a Command

Men Are Always to Pray and Not Faint

Sophia L. Garcia

Copyright © 2018 Sophia L. Garcia.

All rights reserved. No part of this book may be used or reproduced by any means, graphic, electronic, or mechanical, including photocopying, recording, taping or by any information storage retrieval system without the written permission of the author except in the case of brief quotations embodied in critical articles and reviews.

Scripture taken from the King James Version of the Bible.

Scripture taken from the New King James Version®. Copyright © 1982 by Thomas Nelson. Used by permission. All rights reserved.

Scripture taken from The Message. Copyright © 1993, 1994, 1995, 1996, 2000, 2001, 2002. Used by permission of NavPress Publishing Group.

Scripture quotations marked (NLT) are taken from the Holy Bible, New Living Translation, copyright © 1996, 2004, 2007 by Tyndale House Foundation. Used by permission of Tyndale House Publishers, Inc., Carol Stream, Illinois 60188. All rights reserved.

WestBow Press books may be ordered through booksellers or by contacting:

WestBow Press
A Division of Thomas Nelson & Zondervan
1663 Liberty Drive
Bloomington, IN 47403
www.westbowpress.com
1 (866) 928-1240

Because of the dynamic nature of the Internet, any web addresses or links contained in this book may have changed since publication and may no longer be valid. The views expressed in this work are solely those of the author and do not necessarily reflect the views of the publisher, and the publisher hereby disclaims any responsibility for them.

Any people depicted in stock imagery provided by Getty Images are models, and such images are being used for illustrative purposes only. Certain stock imagery © Getty Images.

ISBN: 978-1-9736-2537-7 (sc)
ISBN: 978-1-9736-2538-4 (hc)
ISBN: 978-1-9736-2536-0 (e)

Library of Congress Control Number: 2018904375

Print information available on the last page.

WestBow Press rev. date: 07/10/2018

I dedicate this book to two of my favorite guys: David and Jonathan, my children. Mommy loves you so much, and I pray that the prayer mantle that's on my life transfers to your lives. I pray that you guys will grow up to know that prayer is essential, and whatever you do, put God first. One day both of you will understand why I bring you to early morning, noonday, and all-night prayer. I have shared my testimony with you both that I was told not to have children after my first child died. Indeed, you guys are a miracle. God kept his word.

Contents

Foreword ix
Acknowledgments xi
Preface xv

Chapter 1: Why Pray? 1
Chapter 2: Silent Prayer 29
Chapter 3: Power of Prayer 51
Chapter 4: Intercessory Prayer 73
Chapter 5: What's the Cost of Your Worship? 99
Chapter 6: Silent No More 111

Different Prayer Postures 125
Balancing the equation 127
Scripture References 129
Endnotes 133

Foreword

Is it an Option or a Command? This is the question that is fundamentally answered about prayer in this book.

"In all armies it is unity of will and purpose which assures victory over the enemy". Fables, Aesop

We all are being challenged in this insightful read, to step up to the plate and to use one of the most neglected weapons of our spiritual army, prayer. We must unite in will and purpose to know that prayer is not the responsibility of a few, but the privilege of all that believe in Jesus Christ. Jesus said in Luke 18:1 "Men ought to always pray and not to faint. In this book Sophia, challenges us to return to the power, the weapon and the need of prayer to all and not just to the labeled "Intercessor". As you read this practical aide which comes from the writer's passion for prayer, you will be assisted in how to balance the emotions of not always getting an answer to the rational understanding that prayer moves you not God. Teaching us to wait in prayer will then began to govern your behavior in moments that we feel we are not reaching God. Each talking point ends with a prayer that you can echo and from that begin to build your own style and voice of prayer. All religions believe and practice some form and rituals to prayer, but we who walk in truth must never turn the principle of weakness being able to have access to strength as some badge of honor we wear, but we must see prayer as submission to God's will in the earth. Drawing to God through the intimacy of prayer, protects us, transforms us and brings us into greater revelation of our God and ourselves. So read, pray and practice these easy but yet profound steps and begin to see a paradigm shift in your walk with God and your understanding of prayer.

Bishop Anthony W. Gilyard

Acknowledgments

I want to first give honor to my Lord and Savior Jesus Christ. You are amazing. Words cannot express my gratitude. I appreciate you giving me this assignment and anointing me to pray.

To my wonderful husband, who goes above and beyond to make us happy—Freed, you are the world's most fabulous husband, and I appreciate everything you have done for the kids and me. Thanks for the last twenty years. Although every day was not what we had hoped, we have been keeping the promise "till death do us part." I give God all the glory for keeping us together. Thanks for getting on my nerves. You keep me praying. I know I drive you crazy, but prayer has continued to bring us closer.

To the world's kindest mom, Beverly Mattis-Brown, I love you dearly. I have yet to meet someone who is caring and giving like you. Although you did not bring me up in church weekly, I thank God you sent me with the neighbors sometimes and a seed was planted. I also thank God that he saved you and gave you what I like to call the power gifts: prayer and revelation. I am so grateful for your love and prayers. It does not matter what time I call. You are always ready to pray. Although we did not have the mother-daughter relationship that some people have, I know you have never stopped loving me. I thank you for being my mother, and I thank God for binding us together years later. I love you so much.

To the world's greatest, New Jersey's bravest, and BJCF's finest pastor, Bishop Anthony W. Gilyard. How can I say thanks? You have believed in me since day one. I never had to prove myself to you. You knew there was ministry in me, and you took a big chance. I love you, Bishop. You are indeed a man after God's own heart. You exemplify the love of Jesus. When I was on the road to backsliding, and wanted to give up on myself, you spoke life back to me, and I am eternally grateful. I genuinely believe you tricked me into ministry. You told Sister Karleen to call me and set up a meeting.

I came into the office and asked, "Am I in trouble?"

You said, "Sit down."

And while we were talking, you asked if I was ready to start helping with praying in the church. Being excited about prayer, I said, "*Yes!*"

And you said, "Okay, on Sunday I want you to wear your white dress. I am going to consecrate you as a minister in training and the church intercessory prayer person."

I was a wreck from Thursday to Sunday. Writing this brings me back to that day, and I still get nervous thinking about it.

To my spiritual mothers.

Joanne Alexandra Eld. Joe—gone but not forgotten. I miss you so much. Words cannot express how much. You were such an inspiration in my life. I miss our being together, being silly, and just being us.

Beverley Kemp—thanks for letting me be a part of your family. I love you.

Mary Cochran—you are such an example to me. You love me in spite of my frailty. You are not afraid to rebuke, instruct, and correct me in love. Thanks for keeping me in line and making sure I stay prayed up. It's almost as if I have to dot every I and cross every T. I love you so much, Ma.

To my spiritual sisters.

Darenda Mays and Karleen Hull—we took a journey together that I will never forget. At one point on this route, we were considered "the three Hebrew boys." And Minister Sherabim Allen—or as I call you, Powerhouse—you were an inspiration in my life before God bonded us together. Lisa Bennett, Michelle Jackman, Michelle States, and Althea Womack, I have nothing but love for you guys. Thanks for being there when I needed you most. Chenyce Allen and Annette Manning-Julien, my fasting partners, thanks for your willingness to serve. Cindy Newsome, you were a godsend when most people thought I did not hear the voice of God because spiritually I was young in the faith. You believed in me and helped pray me through.

Preface

I wrote this book because of my passion for prayer. As a licensed minister over the intercessory prayer department, my desire is for people everywhere to understand that prayer is one of the essential elements of Christianity. It is an act of worship, and it plays a vital role in the church. I believe many of God's people do not understand what it means to really pray and what prayer can do. One of my great desires is to maintain a successful prayer life even though that is not an easy task for me. I try my best every day not to leave God out of the equation of my complicated life. Prayer is a personal choice, and if you don't make up your mind to pray, you will never do it. Having a prayer life is not something that just happens; you have to stay focused and make time to pray.

The most significant thing about prayer is that you can pray anywhere and anytime. I pray this book helps you in your walk with God, and I hope you understand that you don't have to have a title or hold a position in the church to pray. All you need is a sincere heart and an open spirit to talk to God. One of God's greatest desires is to have fellowship with you. God, the Creator of the universe, wants to commune with you. He wants your undivided attention at some point in your day.

My encouragement to you is to reverence the Creator of the universe, to put him first, and to honor him with your life. I pray that while you are reading this book, the Holy Spirit will ignite the fire of God inside you and your life will never be the same. I command every hindering force that will distract you and keep you from prayer to go now in Jesus's name. I pray the Holy Spirit will arrest your spirit and give you the courage to go to the throne in faith because "God has not given you the spirit of fear but of love, power, and a sound mind" (2 Timothy 1:7 NKJV). I bind the spirit of fear and intimidation, and I lose the spirit of faith and courage in your life today. From this day forward, let prayer become the air that you breathe, the habit you don't want to let go of, and the lifeline you will use, not just when it's needed but at all times.

Circle the correct answer.

Q1: How should one pray?
- A. Kneeling
- B. Sitting
- C. Standing
- D. Walking
- E. Lying prostrate
- F. All the above

Q2: Where should one pray?
- A. In church
- B. At home
- C. Anywhere
- D. In stores
- E. Silently
- F. All the above

Q3: When should one pray?
- A. In sickness
- B. In times of trouble
- C. Sometimes
- D. Morning only
- E. Only at night
- F. At all times

Q4: Who should we pray for?
- A. Unsaved
- B. Believers only
- C. Government
- D. Family members
- E. Strangers

F. Everyone

Q5: Whose name should we pray in?
   A. Father's name
   B. Pastor's name
   C. Church's name
   D. Mother's name
   E. All the above
   F. Jesus's name

I pray that the answers to those questions will be answered as you read through this book.

Acronym for Prayer

Pray to God.
Read his word.
And encourage
Yourself
Every day,
Regardless of the situation!

What prayer is not!

> Two men went up into the temple to pray; the one a Pharisee, and the other a publican. The Pharisee stood and prayed thus with himself, God, I thank thee, that I am not as other men are, extortioners, unjust, adulterers, or even as this publican. I fast twice in the week, I give tithes of all that I possess. (Luke 18:10 KJV)

What prayer is!

> And the publican, standing afar off, would not lift up so much as his eyes unto heaven, but smote upon his breast, saying, God be merciful to me a sinner. I tell you, this man went down to his house justified rather than the other: for everyone that exalteth himself shall be abased; and he that humbleth himself shall be exalted. (Luke 18:11 KJV)

1

Why Pray?

> And he spake a parable unto them to this end, that
> men ought always to pray, and not to faint.
> —Luke 18:1 (KJV)

We pray because God is sovereign, and he answers prayer. Refusing to pray is a deliberate act of disobedience. When we don't pray, we are only saying to God, "I can handle my business for today." If we are not walking in the principles of his word and obeying his command, it is not a guarantee that he will answer our prayers. Many of us wonder how we can have a better prayer life or how we can pray like other people, not realizing that prayer is just talking with Jesus. Under any circumstances, prayer formulates our thoughts and causes us to make wise decisions. Prayer is not an option; whether we want to pray or not, prayer is the answer to humans' dilemmas. You don't have to pray in a fancy way, and you don't have to pray politically correctly, but prayer must be authentic because you are praying to a holy God. Prayer is not just for people with a title, because sometimes titles replace the relationship one has with God, so keep in mind that nothing and no one should take the place of our prayer time with God. Prayer is mandatory, and it must become the driving force of everything we do in our personal walks with God. Because prayer causes us to build on our relationships with our Lord and Savior, Jesus Christ, it should be the foundation of a believer's walk.

What is prayer? Prayer is the sincerity of the heart articulating one's speech to our heavenly Father, who is listening, and we must patiently wait for him to respond. "Then you will call on me and come and pray to me, and I will listen to you" (Jeremiah 29:12 NIV). People gather in churches, synagogues, and even their homes and pray day and night. Sadly, some of them are praying to a deity we don't know or a being we cannot relate to because they have no relationship with Jesus. Therefore, it is so important to know who Jesus is because knowing Jesus Christ gives us access to the throne. "Let us go boldly to the throne of Grace to obtain mercy and find grace in a time of need" (Hebrews 4:15–16 NKJV). Jesus gave his followers an invitation to freely express themselves through prayer by coming to his throne with confidence, knowing that we can experience his compassion toward a miscreant, which is available every time we express our concerns.

> Prayer is the sincerity of the heart articulating one's speech to our heavenly Father

Praying is fundamental, and the fundamental of prayer is twofold. First, prayer shows our dependence upon God. When we seek his face in the morning by releasing our concerns to him, we demonstrate that we trust he knows what he's doing. Second, God will talk back to us by bringing a song or scripture to our minds. For this reason, one should not rush out of prayer or hurry God because he is not at our mercy; we are the ones who need him. When we rush out of prayer without waiting for God to speak to us, we could miss out on a revelation or divine impartation. In prayer, God can show us a great idea, a business plan, or the way in which he wants us to start the ministry he has placed inside of us. He said, "Call upon me, and I will answer thee and show thee great and mighty things, which thou know not" (Jeremiah 33:3 KJV). This generation must develop an appetite for God and prayer because he has a desire to communicate with his creation, whom he loves. God had a conversation with himself about us in Genesis 1:26 (KJV). "Let's make man into our own image." God is a talking being, and his ideas are unlimited. He is looking for people he can trust and who are willing to seek him in prayer. Prayer will activate the information that God uploaded into your spirit when you were conceived.

When God created Adam, Eve was also created. So, when God was ready to manifest Eve, God put Adam to sleep. Although Adam was asleep, he knew what God had done because he said that Eve was "bones of my bones and flesh of my flesh." When God went to Adam to ask him to name the animals he had created, Adam had no problem completing this task because God had created his mind. (Read Genesis 2: 19-20) Adam was part of God's spirit because he stayed in constant communication with him. However, when Adam disobeyed God by eating fruit from the tree of knowledge of good and evil, Adam exchanged one of the most influential elements he had with God: fellowship, the inseparable bond. Because of the lust of the eye, he lost contact with the divine mind, and God began to look for Adam not because he was lost but because he was out of place with his relationship with God (Genesis 2:4—3:24 KJV). This is a prime example of the unconditional love

God has for his children. His affection for us is immense, and even when we fall short of his grace, he wants to hear from us.

Every one of God's children is responsible for communicating with him through prayer. According to Bishop Anthony W. Gilyard, God is concerned about our well-being. He wants us to have lives of abundance, lives in which we are whole, complete, and functional. If we lead lives that are dysfunctional and unstable, our prayer habits will suffer. Not praying would lead us to lose every battle in our lives. Although the battle belongs to the Lord, we must remember that prayer is our best defense and God's way of giving us victory. When you have a prayer life, you will have power with God and authority over the enemy. Prayer will manifest the favor of God, command the enemy to back up, and return the people of God to their ordained place.

God gives each of us a spiritual gift, and all of us are talented, but we are not aware of what God wants us to do with the gifts he has given us. (Read Romans 11:29 KJV.)

Many of you may feel intimidated because of how God is using someone else, and you may wonder why you are not the one chosen to carry out that mission. God is used to doing his will, especially in your local church. Instead of worrying about why you were not chosen to be the one exercising your gift, take it to God through prayer. Worrying opens the door to self-pity, which invites the enemy to come in and torment your mind, planting in you the feeling that God doesn't care. But God does care, and when you feel abandoned or isolated, as if people do not recognize that you are gifted and have something to offer, you can rest assured that God is preparing you for a higher task.

> *Worrying opens the door to self-pity, which invites the enemy to come in and torment your mind*

The church you attend to worship him may just be the training ground for this task, or perhaps it's not the time for you to be released and go forth into ministry. "Be anxious for nothing, but with prayer and supplication make your request be known unto God" (Philippians 4:6 NKJV).

Prayer promotes the enhancement of growth, and it will enhance the gift of God that he has entrusted you with, so you don't have to worry if he's going to use you. All you need to do is to place yourself in prayer and allow him to equip and empower you for his service. In Luke 18:1, the scripture did not give us any indication of why the widow in this verse was pleading her cause; maybe her husband had died and left the land in his name. Also, he probably had an outstanding debt, and she did not have a kinsman redeemer, so she took matters into her own hands because her enemy wanted to take everything away from her. (Read Leviticus 25:25 KJV.) We see a similarity in 2 Kings 4:1 (KJV) with the widow and the prophet Elisha. However, this widow's persistence shows that she knew her rights, because the apostles appointed men in Acts 6 to make sure widows from Greek and Hebrew backgrounds were taken care of during the daily distribution of food. Though Jesus spoke of parable, he emphasized to his disciples that if an unjust judge could find it in his heart to be fair to this widow because of her persistence, your heavenly Father will turn his heart toward you more if you continue to pray for a spouse who needs help instead of judging him or her because he or she is not at the same level that you experience Christ. Pray for your child who's rebelling against the plan God has for his or her life. Pray for that loved one who has an illness, for your local

> *Prayer promotes the enhancement of growth, and it will enhance the gift of God that he has entrusted you with*

church family, and most of all for your leaders. "For with God, nothing is impossible" (Luke 1:37 KJV). Jesus wanted his disciples to know that they could not give up on prayer just because prayer had not yielded the request from God yet. God might not give the answer we are looking for on the first day. But if we are persistent, things can change; we just should trust God and allow him to work out what we are not able to figure out.

Personal Testimony

I used to wonder, *When is God going to use me and my gifts in the ministry that he has called me to do?* After all, God told me to leave my former church and placed me in a new church: Bethlehem Judah Christian Fellowship. I was so excited and was ready for what God wanted me to do. But I was heartbroken because the departure from one ministry for another is not always understood by the people you no longer worship with at the same church. Within a year's time, I found out that I was three months pregnant. I was disappointed because the ministry was what was in my heart, and my pregnancy would have been a setback. But my pregnancy was not a setback; I learned that my first call was to minister to my family and not the church. So many of God's people are frustrated because they don't know their place in the body of Christ. I was impatient and lacked the understanding of being called by God. However, it was during my pregnancy that God dealt with my broken spirit and the issue of my heart.

I was diagnosed as having a high-risk pregnancy and needed to be on bed rest for the duration of the pregnancy. After I gave birth to my second son, a voice spoke to me and said, "Relax. The church was in the same position when you went out on maternity leave; your call is not running away from you. Just as you were on bed rest during your pregnancy, you are now on bed rest in the spirit. You are in a critical place and need healing." Not only did I need emotional healing, but my spirit also required healing. That's when it dawned on me that I was not ready to do ministry because I was emotionally unstable, which would have affected me spiritually. I then would have ministered out of my brokenness and not from being whole. Then I heard a voice say to me one day, "The same way I helped you during your pregnancy, I am going to help you through this process spiritually."

Prayer

Father, I pray for my brother or sister who is reading this book right now, and I ask that you equip and empower him/her for your service. Let him/her know that the promises of God and what he/she is going through are just a process for your glory. I command the gift of God to be awakened on the inside of you in Jesus's name. Amen.

Need for Salvation

> All have sinned, and come short of the glory of God. (Romans 3:23 KJV)

No one is above prayer, and everyone needs prayer. Prayer increases confidence and allows us to accept the things we cannot change, but unfortunately, some people think the way to get rid of their problem is to commit suicide. On April 19, 2017, according to Fox News, Aaron Hernandez, the former New England Patriots star who was convicted of murder in 2015, killed himself in his prison cell, officials said. Ironically, it was reported that he had the scripture John 3:16 written on his forehead. I believe that God was dealing with Hernandez's heart and giving him a chance to repent. He had the right motive but the wrong approach if he was the one who took his own life. Suicide was never a part of God's plan for humanity.

God's plan for humankind is universal. "For God so loved the world that he gave his only begotten son that whosoever believe in him should not perish but have everlasting life" (John 3:16 KJV). Jesus gave his life, so you don't have to take yours. He exemplifies God's love on the cross, so my prayer today is that you accept Jesus Christ and walk in the newness of life. "This means that anyone who belongs to Christ has become a new person. The old life is gone; a new life has begun!" (2 Corinthians 5:17 NLT). It's crucial that we accept the new life. There is a thin line between life and death, and that thin line represents accepting or rejecting God; either way, one day you are going to meet Jesus, and it's all up to you. You can meet him as a judge or a savior; the choice is yours. Each of us has to stand before the judgment seat of Christ and give an account for the way we live our lives on the earth. For a person to experience the new birth, one must become "born again" by accepting Jesus Christ as Lord and Savior. One cannot experience salvation because one's family member accepted Christ; one must repent by asking Jesus for forgiveness.

> *Each of us has to stand before the judgment seat of Christ and give an account for the way we live our lives on the earth.*

God wants everyone to come to a genuine knowledge of Jesus Christ. Prayer is the tool the Holy Spirit uses to soften people's hearts and allows them to yield to the power of God. Prayer is the wireless connection with direct access to a Holy God. "For it is by grace you have been saved, through faith—and this is not from yourselves; it is the gift of God" (Ephesians 2:8 NIV). Jesus came to earth for one purpose only. His objective was to restore humanity to its original state, back to a relationship with God. He did just that on the cross, and while he was on the cross, he prayed, "Father, forgive them for they know not what they do" (Luke 23:34 KJV).

The book of Leviticus reveals that the Israelites had to bring offerings for the Lord, which can be described as atonement for sin. The sacrifice was offered up as a substitute for the life of the people because of their disobedience in that God would turn away his wrath. The fact that Jesus came and bore our sins and suffered on the cross means we are no longer slaves to sin because "without the shedding of blood there is no remission for sin'" (Hebrews 9:22 KJV). Therefore, we are no longer under the dispensation of law because Jesus Christ's death turned away God's wrath. We are now under the dispensation of grace. "Grace is God's unmerited favor"—even though we deserve nothing from the creator, he extends his hands of mercy toward us every morning.

Personal Testimony

Before I gave my heart to the Lord Jesus Christ, I was suicidal. At the age of twenty-four, I was married and seven months pregnant, and I gave birth to a premature baby girl who lived for only two months. I felt unworthy and began to think God did not love me, telling myself that nothing good would happen in my life. So, one day, while I was home alone reasoning within myself and bringing up issues from my past, I became very depressed and thought suicide was the only way out. I got a bottle of pills and a cup of water, and before taking the pills, a voice spoke to me saying there was no forgiveness of suicide. But there was no one else in the apartment, and because I was a religious person, I said out loud,

"God, if you are real and you are out there, please come into my heart and save me." At that moment, I gave my heart to Jesus.

When I am not in church, occasionally I urge people to give their hearts to God. I know people do not have to repent only in church to have a relationship with God. Prayer invites God to knock at people's hearts. So, go ahead and start praying. You don't have to pray a great prayer; just pray the prayer of repentance; ask God to forgive you for all your sins because Jesus's death on the cross grants you access to the kingdom if you repent and continue to abide in him.

Prayer

Heavenly Father, I pray for those who are contemplating suicide right now, in the name of Jesus. I rebuke the plan of the enemy. Father, let your love reach the hearts, minds, and souls of men, women, and children across the nation, in Jesus's name. Amen.

Self-Examination

What people need today is your love and not your judgment. "Don't pick on people, jump on their failures, or criticize their faults unless, of course, you want the same treatment. That critical spirit has a way of boomeranging" (Matthew 7:1–3 MSG).

The scripture revealed that "Jabez called out to the God of Israel: 'If only You would bless me, extend my border, let Your hand be with me, and keep me from harm, so that I will not cause any pain.' And God granted his request." This prayer of Jabez is short and powerful and found in 1 Chronicles 4:10 (HCSB). It teaches us that Jabez examined himself when he asked God to bless him and keep him from harm so that he would not mess it up for everyone else. He knew that his mom had had a hard time during her pregnancy, so she called him what she had experienced. But Jabez refused to live by the label of his name, and he went to the one who had the power to change his situation. He understood through prayer that his motive had to be right for God to bless him and enlarge his borders, so he approached the throne of grace in humility, and God granted him his petition. Jabez wanted to be emotionally stable so that he could handle the blessings of God upon his life. "For if a man thinks he is something, when he is nothing, he deceives himself. But let each one test his own work, and then his reason to boast will be in himself alone" (Galatians 6:3–4 NIV).

When it comes to self-examination, our first line of defense is to put ourselves on the altar before God and allow him to pull off the layers of pretense so we can be real with him. Otherwise, our prayers are in vain. Self-examination helps to deflate our egos and give us a heart for God. If we don't examine ourselves, the enemy will cause us a life of deception wherein we think we don't need prayers. Just because you have a great prayer life does not mean you don't need prayer. We must recognize when we need prayer and reach out to others to pray for us. That shows humility.

> *Self-examination helps to deflate our egos and give us a heart for God*

Self-examination is crucial to our spiritual walk with God. We will not be able to have a lifestyle of prayer and have the power of God operating in our lives by walking in our flesh and being carnal. Carnality will diminish your prayer life and cause the light of Christ in you to be dim. "Therefore, since we are surrounded by such a huge crowd of witnesses to the life of faith, let us strip off every weight that slows us down, especially the sin that easily trips us up, and let us run with endurance the race God has set before us" (Hebrews 12:1 NLT). Notice that the scripture says "weight" and "sin." That means some things we do are not necessarily sins but add to sin's weight. Thus, we have to be able to differentiate what we are carrying in our spirit because if we are not careful, people's burdens will become weight. And if we go around discussing other people's business instead of praying, that weight will become a sin. This will then cause us to be distracted when praying, and our prayers will have no value or meaning. We will feel as if our prayers are bouncing off the wall.

We cannot listen to gossip, and we must not entertain that spirit that draws us away from our prayer time with God. When we are not praying and fellowshipping with God, we leave ourselves open to sin. Sin is always knocking at the door of our heart, and if we are not praying, we are saying, "Holy Ghost, let me answer the door today." When sin is present in our lives, it will cause us to be unstable in our walk with God. If you are called to pray, you cannot be emotionally unstable. We have to be experienced soldiers in the army of the Lord, always ready to battle with God. God needs us, and we need him.

Many of us are called to pray, and because we do not understand the call, we get frustrated and think that God does not hear our prayers and that we don't have the connections as other people do. In ministry, especially in prayer, we cannot compare ourselves to anyone. Although we are in a race, this race is spiritual; it's not a competition. God has assigned each of us a different task, but all of us need to have a lifestyle of prayer. If we are called to pray, we need to let the Holy Ghost develop us and give us the wisdom on how to deal with the people he assigned us. We are to be patient and long-suffering because if we are not careful, we will miss out on the great privilege God has given to us to pray and birth someone to the next dimension. There is a mantle of prayer that believers can obtain through prayer, but we must make the sacrifice to pray and ask God to release it.

Moses was a great intercessor who had the prayer mantle, but unfortunately, he let his emotions get in the way and missed out on the promised land because he did not deal with the spirit of anger. The spirit of anger must be dealt with because anger is contagious, and when you are angry, you influence people with your negative vibes. Otherwise, it can prevent you from getting to your ordained place with God. You will be going through the routine and traditions of prayer but not truly interceding. Moses allowed the people he was leading to get under his skin when he decided to take the matter into his own hands. God told him to speak to the rock, and he struck it.

> Then Moses raised his arm and struck the rock twice with his staff. Water gushed out, and the community and their livestock drank. But the LORD said to Moses and Aaron, "Because you did not trust in me enough to honor me as holy in the sight of the Israelites, you will not bring this community into the land I give them." (Numbers 20:11–12 NIV)

There are many people whom God has anointed to intercede. Some of us let our struggles in the flesh get in the way, and we come up with excuses for why we cannot pray. This causes us to live in fear because we are afraid someone will call on us to pray in a public setting. When we are called to an assignment, it is our responsibility to make sure we adjust our schedule and make time for God's work. We

> *Some of us let our struggles in the flesh get in the way, and we come up with excuses for why we cannot pray.*

will not get anywhere in life spiritually or naturally without disciplining ourselves and making the sacrifice for our ministry, dream, or business come to fruition. Prayer, just like everything else, needs to be worked on. The more you condition your mind and make time for God, the more he will increase your capacity to complete the assignment. Thus, let us take inventory of ourselves and ask God to help us so we won't miss the opportunity for greatness. Don't miss your moment with God. If you lose your passion for prayer because it seems you are praying and nothing is changing, don't be discouraged; just remember that a year to us might be a day to God. He's also not moved by emotion; he moves on faith. So, ask God to forgive you for being slothful and start over. If you are not a person who likes to pray, start giving God a few minutes in the morning, during the day, and in the evening, and you will be surprised at how much your communication with him increases. Over time, you will get a better understanding of how important prayer is because now you will build on the relationship, and you will want to share every aspect of your life with him.

If God has been dealing with you about prayer, if he has woken you up for the past three nights in the middle of the night but you say to yourself, "I don't know how to pray," just start talking. He wants to partner with you so you can help carry out his plan on Earth.

If God's chosen people will forget about themselves for a minute, an hour, or even a day to seek God on behalf of our world's crises, not our problems, and turn from our evil ways, we will begin to see the manifestation of prayer. What's going on in the world does matter, but prayer can break through any barrier and cause the enemy to flee for a season.

Personal Testimony

About two years after I received salvation, I was at home cleaning, and a verse from scripture came to me: "For if a man cannot manage his own household, how can he take care of God's church?" (1 Timothy 3:5 NIV). Of course, I am optimistic, so I tried to reason with God. I began to say, "God, I'm not a leader, so why are you saying this to me?" A couple of years later, I thought I understood the interpretation. I became the assistant Sunday school superintendent at my former church, so I made sure my house was clean before I went to the house of God. It may sound funny now, but what some of us do is take the scripture out of context. God knows that during that season, I probably did not care, and my house was a mess, but God wanted me to keep it clean. Obedience goes a long way.

But I must admit, today I understand that I cannot be a leader in the house of God, better yet an intercessor, and not know how to rule my own spirit. We must practice self-control and examine ourselves before going before a holy God. I have learned that without releasing the people or things I am carrying in my heart, I will not be successful in prayer. What I mean by "not successful" is that my prayers will not reach heaven or get an answer. I am a witness to what God can do in prayer when we release the burdens from our hearts. When God removes the hurt and pain, you will begin to worship freely and experience his magnificent presence.

Prayer

Heavenly Father, I ask in the name of Jesus that you search me and remove everything that will hinder my prayer today. I pray that you will strengthen my faith and cause me to believe so I can expect a breakthrough and deliverance right now in prayer. I believe it to be so in Jesus's name.

If you are sincere in your prayers and believe, what you prayed for will happen. Just have faith.

Prayer Is Personal

Most people want their relationship to work, but sadly, many quit during the dating process. As believers, we are the bride of Christ, and a bride does not act as if she is dating her husband because she is now committed to him. When you are dating, it is easy to change partners. We can see a relationship as casual while looking for the "right" person we are compatible with. As believers, our prayer lives with God cannot be casual as if we are dating him. God does not want to date; he wants commitment. And if we are going to be committed to God, we must get personal with him. Prayer will move us from being familiar with God to a place of oneness with him. When you are in love with someone, you feel the urgency and the longing to be with him or her.

> God does not want to date; He wants commitment

Every moment and every chance we get to be in God's presence, we must use the time wisely because he's not only our creator, he's our Father. It is an insult to God when his children do not obey his commands. The truth of the matter is, when the bride of Christ refuses to acknowledge her husband (Christ, the head of the church) in prayer, she is only telling God, "I got this, and if I am approached with any challenges today, then I will need your assistance." Some people see prayer as the way out after their plans fall apart, they cried out to God and made vows that they cannot keep, but prayer must be our first intuition because we are fortunate to see another day. Prayer is our covering, so if we are not praying, we leave ourselves more vulnerable to the attacks of the enemy. Not praying is like going on vacation and forgetting to lock the doors to your house. It's a high possibility when you get back home your house will be vandalized. Don't forget to lock your spiritual doors today by praying. Failing to lock your spiritual doors will cause your spirit to be vulnerable when situations arise. If you close your spiritual doors by praying when circumstances present themselves, you will be affected, but your spirit will not be broken to the point of no recovery.

One of my greatest desires is to be able to maintain my personal prayer life with my heavenly Father. While that's not an easy thing for me to do, I have learned that the key to the maintenance of a successful prayer life is being consistent on a regular basis and spending time in God's word. When you communicate with God daily, you are building an everlasting relationship. If you do not speak to God, you will not be able to distinguish his voice from the enemy's voice. By meditating on God's word, you will get to know more about him on a personal level. Not only will you get to know him better, but it also makes it easier for you to have a conversation with him. Prayer is not just getting on your knees, but it's the concept of building a relationship with God.

Each time we read the Bible and see Jesus, the man of impeccable character, encounter someone in a situation that needs a miracle, he does not struggle to pray. He fearlessly proclaims the word or gives explicit instructions because of the connection he has with the Father. At the tomb of Lazarus, Jesus did not have to pray; he

> The key to the maintenance of a successful prayer life is being consistent on a regular basis and spending time in God's word.

could have just called Lazarus forth. But he prayed to show the critics that God had sent him and that he was the will of God (John 11:42 KJV). He was bold enough to say, "Father, I know you always hear me," indicating unbroken fellowship. He had confidence and assurances because of his relationship. Jesus did not just operate in the earth realm because he was God's Son; he exerted God's will because he consistently acknowledged his father.

You can get to a place in God where you don't have to pray about some situations; you can just speak the word. Prayer is getting in your unique meeting place in the morning and allowing your spirit to send a signal of intimacy to the Father. Prayer is a personal thing. As much as we love to call a prayer meeting in church—and it's beautiful to get a group of people to pray together—we find Jesus in the scripture on many occasions praying alone. And he went out before daybreak. Jesus usually prayed before he started his day; that's why he was so successful in his earthly ministry. When we read the synoptic gospels, we find that on many occasions, Jesus didn't have to pray for the sick; he would just speak or send the word because he was already prayed up.

Jesus made prayer his priority. It was not just a part of his life; it was his lifestyle. And because prayer was his lifestyle, the power of God flowed through him. Many of God's children want the power of God to manifest in their lives without investing time in prayer and the word of God. The disciples recognized the potential that worked in the life of Jesus and must have felt it had something to do with his prayer, so they asked him to teach them how to pray (Luke 11:1 KJV). They knew walking with Jesus and seeing him

> *Many of God's children want the power of God to manifest in their lives without investing time in prayer and the word of God.*

performing miracles had something to do with his prayer life. Prayer was the backbone of Jesus's ministry, and it should be the foundation believers stand on.

Prayer was not only important to Jesus, but it was also personal. In Matthew 6:6 KJV, Jesus gives an illustration of prayer. "But when you pray, enter into your closet." Going into a closet doesn't mean you should go into a closet literally, but you should have a place set aside where you can have your personal moments with God, shutting out all distractions and bringing your mind, body, and spirit under the subjection of the Holy Ghost.

God wants you to be personal with him. He wants your undivided attention so he can shape your life. Prayer is like a sewing machine by which each stitch brings the material to the form of the person who was measured to fit the garment. So, when you pray, you can imagine yourselves being in the fitting room of God, where your lives can be molded into the life of Christ. We are not to look at prayer as a religious duty set aside for pastors, evangelists, or those in leadership positions. Instead, we are to see prayer as an opportunity to receive our daily bread—God's word for our lives (Matthew 6:11 KJV).

Jesus told his disciples that whatever you need, you can ask his father and he will give it to you according to his will (paraphrasing John 14:13–14 KJV). Brothers and sisters, you do not have to go outside of the kingdom covenant to get what you need from God because God is our provider. When we read Genesis 22, we find out that God tested Abraham by asking him to sacrifice his only son. God already had the ram provided for Abraham to sacrifice instead of his son; it's just that the ram was not yet revealed unto Abraham until the appointed time. There are times in our lives when we pray to God, and he will not reveal the answer until the appointed time, so do not lose hope; just keep on praying until you get to a mature place in your life where you will comprehend that some things are just a test. God does not promote his children until they pass the test and are ready for the next task.

Prayer is a part of the study tool you need to pass the test of life. While Jesus was on earth, he was able to pass every test because he was in constant communication with his Daddy. Jesus used the tool of prayer that the Father had given him. Prayer will connect you to the Father and cause your inner man to gain strength. So, if you are at a place in your life where you feel as if you are drained, take the time to pray and let the Holy Ghost take over so you can build up yourself in it (Jude 1:20 KJV). There is a place where you can get engrossed in prayer. It may not happen overnight, but if you continue to build on your relationship with the Father, I assure you that you will reach the place where there is no limit, and you have unlimited access to the Father in prayer.

Your very souls will be blessed, and you will be able to identify with the psalmist David, who said, "Oh taste and see that the Lord is good" (Psalm 34:8 KJV). Prayer will force you to deal with what you are going through in the difficulties of life. If you are going through something right now, start praying and allow God to lift the burdens on your heart: "Father, I ask that you lift this burden I'm carrying now, in Jesus's name." The situation might not change right away, but you will feel better and be glad that you prayed about it. For example, someone might have offended you with his or her words, but instead of letting the offense get the best of you, bring the situation into prayer. The next time you see that person, you can have a normal conversation because you let go of the offense in prayer. No longer are you holding on to the hurt because you have released it to the Creator.

Some Christians fail to realize that prayer does not exempt us from a life of suffering on our spiritual journey. When we read the scriptures, we find prophets such as Jeremiah and Daniel as well as godly men such as Job and David, who faced much opposition on their walk with God. Although they faced difficult tasks, they never ceased praying and relying on God. The prophet's dependency upon God can encourage us to pray, especially when we find ourselves in difficult circumstances. So, when life throws you a curveball, instead of striking out, pick up the batten of prayer and throw up some praises so you can hit a home run back into his presence.

Our experiences will not only prepare us but also help us to encourage other believers when they are going through their test. Therefore, prayer must become the essential part of your life with Christ. God could have summoned someone else to commune with him, but he has chosen you. He is looking for intimacy with someone who desires his presence and wants to be with him. Right now, you can have alone time with him by committing a few minutes and letting him know how awesome he is. Tell him how beautiful he is, how good he has been to you, and go ahead and love on him.

Prayer elevates our minds and gives us a different perspective on life. If Christians would ever understand the concept of prayer, that it is getting to know God personally, I believe more people would attend prayer services because prayer will give us the perseverance to resist the temptations that this world offers us.

> *Prayer elevates our minds and gives us a different perspective on life.*

Personal Testimony

Prayer is not always easy, and many times I don't feel like praying. But I choose to talk to my heavenly Father because he has been good to me. Sometimes I just tell him about me. I begin to say, "Lord, today I am frustrated, and I ask if you can help me not to walk in my flesh. I don't want to be bothered, so God, you're going to have to help me through this day." Other times I listen to gospel music so the words of the song can minister to my spirit and help me cope with what I'm facing on that day.

Prayer

Father, I pray in the name of Jesus for those who do not feel like praying because of discouragement. Help them to realize they cannot give up on you because of the burden they are carrying. Father, your word says, "You will not give us more than we can bear." Father, I release everything that will slow me down today and not allow me to give you praise. Thank you for hearing and answering my prayer in Jesus's name.

He's Waiting to Hear Your Voice

We can no longer wish to devote more time to him; we must make time for him. Spending time talking to God can no longer be an afterthought; it must be a part of our daily living. When we seek God, he will deal with us on an individual basis, so it doesn't matter who you are, what nationality you are, or what organization you serve in; you can offer up a prayer. Our Father, who sits on the throne in heaven, worshiped by angels, is waiting patiently to hear your voice. Your voice is so unique and valuable to God that he takes the time to listen to you. Psalm 4:1 KJV says, "Hear me when

I call, O God of my righteousness: thou hast enlarged me when I was in distress; have mercy upon me and hear my prayer."

> Listen to my voice in the morning, LORD. Each morning I bring my requests to you and wait expectantly. (Psalm 5:3 NLT)

The body of Christ must understand that God has always had a listening ear to the cries of his children. God has given his children a personal invitation to call upon him. No reservation is needed; he's available twenty-four hours a day, seven days a week, regardless of the situation. The mere fact that he wants to hear from you is an indication that he's willing to do something about your circumstances. In Exodus 3 it was the cry of the children of Israel that caused God to visit Moses while he was attending his father-in-law's sheep on the backside of the desert. God spoke to Moses out of a burning bush and told him he wanted him to deliver his people out of the land of Egyptians

> And the LORD said, I have surely seen the affliction of my people which are in Egypt, and have heard their cry by reason of their taskmasters; for I know their sorrows; And I am come down to deliver them out of the hand of the Egyptians, and to bring them up out of that land unto a good land and a large, unto a land flowing with milk and honey; unto the place of the Canaanites, and the Hittites, and the Amorites, and the Perizzites, and the Hivites, and the Jebusites. Now therefore, behold, the cry of the children of Israel is come unto me: and I have also seen the oppression wherewith the Egyptians oppress them. Come now

therefore, and I will send thee unto Pharaoh, that thou mayest bring forth my people the children of Israel out of Egypt. (Exodus 3:7–10 KJV)

Furthermore, when God used Moses to deliver the children of Israel, he wanted to make sure he stayed in direct communication with him, so he instructed Moses to make a mercy seat and put it above the altar and told him that was the meeting place (Exodus 25:22 KJV). Simply put, I will be waiting to hear your voice.

In 1 Samuel chapter 3, when God called Samuel, he did not realize it was the Lord; instead he ran to Eli. Here is an indication that Samuel did not recognize the voice of God, or perhaps he never heard the voice of God. The scripture states that when Eli perceived that the Lord was calling Samuel; he told him to say, "Here I am Lord your servant heareth." Here, Samuel took heed to Eli's instruction and the next time he heard the voice; he recognized it was the voice of God. He answered "Here I am Lord your servant is listening."

How awesome it is that the God of the universe, your Creator, wants to hear from you anytime and anywhere. You don't have to feel inadequate in prayer or be intimidated because you might not have the right words to say to him. Just cry out. Whatever you say, he knows how to interpret what you mean, so go ahead and share your concerns because whatever bothers you concerns him too.

> Prayer is necessary for your spiritual growth and your personal development. It will break the barriers of limitations.

Prayer is necessary for your spiritual growth and your personal development. It will break the barriers of limitations. When you are praying, you allow the Holy Spirit to take inventory of your life and show you the things that are not pleasing to God. Prayer will sensitize your heart to his voice. Jesus says, "My sheep know my voice, and I know them, and they follow me" (John 10:27 KJV). It is not enough just to hear God's voice; we must also follow his instruction. It takes time to learn God's voice. If we are going to know the voice of God, we must ask him to help us discern his voice in prayer. In prayer, you can ask God to train your spirit to wait in his presence, and his voice will become more distinct to you. Above all, God wants to give you strategic insight on how to operate in the earth realm. Prayer is the invisible line that connects us to the primary source who is God, and when we are not attached to the power supply, we are at a disadvantage.

> One of the disadvantages many believers have when praying is that they do not wait for God to speak back to them in prayer.

One of the disadvantages many believers have when praying is that they do not wait for God to speak back to them in prayer. Though God might not always talk back to you right away, which can be somewhat frustrating, the more you practice waiting in his presence, the more you become familiar with his voice. There are no traffic jams in heaven, so there's no need for you to rush out of his presence. Rushing out of God's presence can cause you significant delay on your spiritual journey with him. Selah in his presence, because prayer will cause you to use wisdom and make a wise decision, especially when faced with difficult circumstances. Spending time with God will cause your spirit to be freer. It causes you to love unconditionally, and it will force you out of your comfort zone. You will be more sensitive to the Spirit of God and be more open so God can use you to bring deliverance to someone else.

Spending time with God is not just for us to grow more spiritual but for us to become more God-conscious. When you are God-conscious, it makes it a little easier to resist the voice of the enemy or even your consciousness (self). Spending time in prayer with God causes you to have joy in your soul because the more you are in the presence of God, the happier you will become. King David experienced the fullness of joy because he spent time in the presence of the Lord. Believers should train themselves to listen to and follow God's perfect will.

"Father, I thank you today for allowing me to be in your presence; help me learn how to listen and follow your perfect will. Guide my steps today, oh Lord, that I may be in your perfect will, in Jesus's name."

God will not lead you astray; he wants the best for you. His best is for you to discover who he is. There is so much for you to know about God. You can begin to experience him by reading his word and praying the scripture back to him, which is one of the best ways to pray. Prayer is like having your phone ring. When we don't answer the call to pray, we miss out on what God wants to say to us, as well as the opportunity to be in his presence and to experience him in another way.

> *God will not lead you astray; he wants the best for you. His best is for you to discover who he is.*

Personal Testimony

I remember one day I was praying and I asked God, "Why are people praying, and there's no change?" Your word says, 'If my people, who are called by my name, will humble themselves and pray and seek my face and turn from their wicked ways, then I will hear from heaven, and I will forgive their sin and will heal their land' (2 Chronicles 7:14 NKJV)." A voice spoke to me and said, "Everyone who is praying is not part of my people." It blew my mind because I knew he creates all people. Also, some of us are his people, but our intentions are wicked, so he is not paying attention to our prayers. This is why we do not see changes in our churches or community because some of God's people are refusing to humble themselves and seek his face.

Prayer

Father, in the name of Jesus, I ask that you allow the person who is reading this now to experience your presence, in Jesus's name! Your presence can be felt anywhere, so God, give this person a yearning in his or her soul for you. Amen!

2

Silent Prayer

Prayer is like having a diary you write in daily; the difference between the two is that one you record on paper and the other you record in heaven.

Being overwhelmed can be harmful both physically and spiritually. Physically, you can be stressed out, which tends to affect your blood pressure. When your blood pressure is high, it can cause other problems in your body. Spiritually, when we are going through our struggles, sometimes we begin to isolate ourselves from family members, run away from the ministry God had called us to do, and give up on our dreams we were once excited about. At that point, we get depressed and frustrated and allow the enemy to disrupt our flow of being in the presence of Almighty God. But it is at that moment that we should run to the house of worship and allow our spirit to connect with God; there, we can go into silent prayer and unleash our heavy burdens.

In 1 Samuel 1, we find a young woman named Hannah. She was married to Elkanah and incapable of conceiving a child. Perhaps because of her barrenness, her husband married another woman named Peninnah, who taunted Hannah regularly because she was aware of Hannah's not being able to conceive. Not surprisingly, this situation created a rivalry between the two women, and Hannah found herself in an unfavorable situation year after year going to the house of the Lord to worship and making sacrifices to God. It must have been a devastating time in Hannah's life because the one thing she wanted—to have a child—she couldn't have. She did not understand that she was going through a temporary setback for a permanent blessing. I imagine Hannah going to bed night after night feeling lonely even though she was married. Hannah was held captive in her own mind by the words of Peninnah; when your enemies know that you are disadvantaged, they will try to keep you in bondage so they can feel better about themselves. I believe Peninnah infuriated her, causing her to feel unworthy and thinking she didn't belong in the family.

> *She did not understand that she was going through a temporary setback for a permanent blessing.*

Nevertheless, Hannah focus begins to shift, and she turned her public humiliation and her own embarrassment into silent prayers.

And it happened, as she continued praying before the Lord, that Eli watched her mouth move, but he did not hear her voice. Therefore, Eli thought she was drunk. Eli said to her, "How long would you be drunk? Put your wine away from you," but Hannah answered, "No, my Lord, I am a woman of sorrowful spirit. I have drunk neither wine nor intoxicating drink but have poured out my soul before the Lord." (1 Samuel 1:12–15 KJV)

Somehow, she must have known God would grant her request that day, and she refused to be the laughingstock among her rivals. She was not going to let her adversary tarnish her reputation anymore. Hannah knew the only person who could open her womb for her to conceive was God, so she took her issue to him. Hannah prayed on purpose and produced a result. So, in chapter 2 (KJV), she was now able to pray the prayer of thankfulness: "My heart rejoices in the Lord, my horn is exalted in the Lord, I smile at my enemies because I rejoice in the God of my salvation."

When you are in a situation where the enemy is provoking you, you don't need to retaliate. Just go into silent prayer. The enemy can't read your mind, nor does he know your thoughts; he can only judge your actions. Hannah made up her mind and refused to let her adversary get the best of her. She went into the house of prayer, carved out space, and silently prayed to her heavenly Father and got a surprising outcome.

> The enemy can't read your mind, nor does he know your thoughts; he can only judge your actions.

You too can reject the games the enemy wants to play with your mind because you don't have what you need from God as yet, and you can have a silent moment with God. Just because you are praying in your heart doesn't mean that God can't hear you. Before Abraham died, he asked his servant to do him a huge favor by finding a wife for his son, Isaac. While Abraham's servant was on his journey, he had to reassure himself that he was able to fulfill the agreement with his master, so he stopped at the well to acknowledge God:

> And I came this day unto the well, and said, 'O Lord God of my master Abraham, if now thou do prosper my way which I go, behold: I stand by the well of water; and it shall come to pass that, when the virgin cometh forth to draw water and I say to her, "Give me, I pray thee, a little water of thy pitcher to drink," and she says to me, "Both drink thou, and I will also draw for thy camels, let the same be the woman whom the Lord hath appointed out for my master's son." And before I had done speaking in mine heart, behold, Rebekah came forth with her pitcher on her shoulder; and she went down unto the well, and drew water: and I said unto her, "Let me drink, I pray thee." (Genesis 24:42–49 KJV)

The servant wanted to accomplish the favor his master had asked him to do. I believe he felt that if this assignment was possible, it had to be done through prayer. After all, he had firsthand experience with how God worked miracles in his master's life. He prayed, and God honored his request. There are times when we will have major decisions to make in our lives. At times, we make our minds up instead of surrendering our will to God and invite him into our decision-making. As we see in this chapter, Abraham's servant left a great example for us to follow. It also teaches us that we must pray and ask God for his wisdom before making decisions because God will allow us to avoid pitfalls in our lives. We must remember when we make a decision, it does not

> *If you want God to direct your steps, you cannot leave him out of the equation of your life.*

only affect us but also the people who are a part of our lives. If you want God to direct your steps, you cannot leave him out of the equation of your life. We need to "trust in the Lord with all our hearts; lean not to our own understanding. In all thy ways acknowledge him, and he shall direct our path" (Proverbs 3:5-6 KJV).

Personal Testimony

I have been in situations where I was publicly embarrassed. I have worked with a company where my boss mistreated me for years. For instance, any assignment that was too difficult for the other employees, she would let them give it to me so I would have to do it, instead of her teaching them how to do it. But I continued to show up to work because it became the norm for me.

I remember one day she said to me, "Sophia, I am not sure why we don't get along. Every night before I go to bed I pray and asked God to help us."

I looked at her in the parking lot and said, "Don't worry about it. God is going to give me a position one day, and I will not treat people the way you treat me."

A couple of years later, that supervisor left, and I was less stressed until a new boss was placed in the position. However, my next supervisor was not able to do the job, so he changed the workflow and gave my workload to one of my staff members. It was easier for him to work with my coworker rather than me because I knew he could not perform his duties. He belittled me in the presence of my staff and created a hostile environment for me so that I could not carry out my job duties. Even when overcoming such obstacles and hostile environments, I still could not understand why God had allowed me to be in this situation, but instead of complaining and foolishly charging God, I sat at my desk and started to pray. I asked God to help me through this situation because his words say that all things work together. I started saying, "God, I don't know why I am in this situation, but it must be for my own good." Immediately the presence of God overshadowed me, and he took the hurt and resentment away. About a month later, manager of the company had a meeting with my boss and me. I felt they were trying to set me up and blame me for a decrease in cash flow, so I sent my pastor a text explaining what was going on at the job. Later that night, I saw him, and he said, "I promise you that if you send your résumé out and get an interview, you will get the job." Within two weeks, God opened a door, and I was able to move on. There are times when God will have us experience unfairness on the job to see how we will respond to the challenges of life.

Sometimes we use beautiful existing prayers, such as the Psalms, hymns, poems, and religious songs; this is "vocal prayer." Other times, we talk to God in silence with only our thoughts and the feelings of our hearts, without any fixed formula; this is "mental prayer." The fact of the matter is depending on what's going on in our lives, we should always include prayer.

Prayer

Father, I pray for those who are going through difficulties at their jobs right now. I pray they will find favor with their bosses and be able to work in a friendly environment. God, even if the environment is not friendly, help us to keep our sanity so you can demonstrate your love so others will see you in us. In Jesus's name, amen.

Be Honest in Prayer

> *If you want your prayer life to be effective, you have to be honest with God.*

You have heard the cliché that honesty is the best policy. If you want your prayer life to be effective, you have to be honest with God. It does not matter how long you have been in church; it doesn't matter if you are the pastor's armor-bearers or the jurisdiction leader. Will God answer your prayer if you are not honest with him? Sadly, dishonesty and deception have influenced the way many people live their lives. We cannot go to God with preconceived notions, thinking we can impress him. God cannot be bribed or manipulated because he knows the intent of your heart.

In 1 Kings 22:1–53 (KJV) we saw that the king of Israel reached out to Jehoshaphat to go to battle with him. However, Jehoshaphat told Ahab that he needed the Lord's blessing, so Ahab gathered about four hundred prophets and asked for their opinions concerning the war they were about to enter. I believe somehow Jehoshaphat felt that something was not right, so he asked for a true prophet. King Ahab sent for the prophet Micaiah, whose word King Ahab did not want to hear. Despite Ahab refusing to hear Micaiah, he warned the king of danger, but the king ignored his instructions and manipulated the people to go to war, thinking that disguising himself by outwitting God would give him victory. In turn Ahab lost his life, and the prophecy of Micaiah came to pass. Also, in John 11 (KJV), we find two sisters who were concerned about their brother, Lazarus, who had a terminal illness. Because they knew Jesus loved him, they tried to manipulate Jesus by sending a letter to emphasize that the one whom he loved was very ill. Instead of the sisters praying for Lazarus's healing, they tried to manipulate Jesus.

If we try to manipulate God, we miss the essence of who he is. We cannot use our influence in life to get what we want if we are not honest about it. We need to pray for what we want instead of trying to bribe God. We may be able to fool everyone else, but we cannot fool God. When we go before a holy God, we have to be open and vulnerable if we want to develop a more significant prayer life. Sometimes our prayers are hindrances because we refuse to let go of grudges, physical discomfort, and our emotional struggles. It could also be that we have offended someone and did not apologize. At this moment, you can ask God to help you to let it go and move on. Unfortunately, if you choose not to repent, you are fighting a losing battle. Psalm 66:18 states, If I regard iniquity in my heart the Lord will not hear" (The Word in Life Study Bible). You can always rebuild your relationship with God if you are honest with him.

> *Sometimes our prayers are hindrances because we refuse to let go of grudges, physical discomfort, and our emotional struggles.*

An example of someone's relationship being restored with God because of honesty was King David after the prophet Nathan confronted him about his adulterous affair with Bathsheba and the murder of her husband. King David could fool the people in his palace, but he was not able to fool God (paraphrasing 2 Samuel 12). When David realized that God knew what he had done, he went to pray and was honest with God. Psalm 51 says (NIV):

> Have mercy on me, O God, according to your unfailing love; according to your great compassion

blot out my transgressions. Wash away all my iniquity and cleanse me from my sin. For I know my transgressions, and my sin is always before me. Against you, you only, have I sinned and done what is evil in your sight; so you are right in your verdict and justified when you judge. Surely I was sinful at birth, sinful from the time my mother conceived me. You desired faithfulness even in the womb; you taught me wisdom in that secret place. Cleanse me with hyssop, and I will be clean; wash me, and I will be whiter than snow. Let me hear joy and gladness; let the bones you have crushed rejoice. Hide your face from my sins and blot out all my iniquity. Create in me a pure heart, O God, and renew a steadfast spirit within me. Do not cast me from your presence or take your Holy Spirit from me. Restore to me the joy of your salvation and grant me a willing spirit, to sustain me. Then I will teach transgressors your ways so that sinners will turn back to you. Deliver me from the guilt of bloodshed, O God, you who are God my Savior, and my tongue will sing of your righteousness. Open my lips, Lord, and my mouth will declare your praise. You do not delight in sacrifice, or I would bring it; you do not take pleasure in burnt offerings. My sacrifice, O God, is a broken spirit; a broken and contrite heart you, God, will not despise. May it please you to prosper Zion, to build up the walls of Jerusalem. Then you will delight in the sacrifices of the righteous, in burnt offerings offered whole; then bulls will be offered on your altar.

Here, King David was very remorseful about his foolish act and asked for God's forgiveness. I believe that sometimes we forget that God is omniscient. Let us walk in truth and be honest with God because no one is perfect, and we are going to make mistakes occasionally. After all, dishonesty keeps our spirits polluted and affects our prayer lives. If you want to grow in your spiritual walk with God, and especially in prayer, you must be open and become vulnerable in his presence. The night before his crucifixion, Jesus made himself vulnerable in the garden of Gethsemane when he prayed. Jesus the Incarnate knew his purpose and what he had come on earth to do. Although he was God, "Instead he gave up his divine privileges: he took the humble position of a slave and was born as a human being. When he appeared in human form" (Philippians 2:7 NLT). Because he gave up his deity, Jesus had a moment of weakness. Perhaps he wanted to change his mind because he knew the pain that he had to face. He would be anxious thinking about the ordeal, yet he was honest with his Father.

This night in prayer was different. He was not praying for God to use him to work miracles; he was telling his Father he wanted to change his mind. He was asking God if there was another way sinners could be saved without him going to the cross. But because of Jesus's submissive and obedient spirit, he prayed, asking God not to meet his need but to accomplish God's plan. And God sent an angel to strengthen him. Jesus expressed himself honestly. He demonstrates that when circumstances arise beyond your control, instead of blaming, be honest with God in prayer by telling him how you feel, and I guarantee you he will send help. He will

> This night in prayer was different. He was not praying for God to use him to work miracles; he was telling his Father he wanted to change his mind.

give you inner strength and peace to sustain you, and you will be able to overcome. When we use chicanery with God, our prayer lives will become contaminated, which will make it easier for us to be critical of other people and not scrutinize our actions. But God is looking for us to be straightforward with him in prayer and will not be judgmental of our prayers if we are honest with him.

Personal Testimony

There was a time in my life that I used to be angry at people and with God because I felt as a child, God had allowed me to experience all different types of abuse. I felt l had been mistreated growing up. Since I was my mother's first child, all the responsibilities fell on my shoulders. Thus, in my marriage, it was hard for me to be submissive until one night, God allowed me to have a dream that I was going to a funeral. A woman in my dream told me I needed to go to the cemetery. When I awoke, I could not understand what the dream meant, so I told it to different people so I could get the interpretation. No one I told could interpret the dream. One day I was sitting in my living room on the couch, and the interpretation came to me. I heard a voice telling me, "If only you would die to your flesh and be submissive to your husband." I spoke to God and asked why my husband is the head; he should be the one to carry out the duties of marriage. I wanted my husband to be submissive to me, but I did not want to submit to him. Then I heard a voice say, "To whom much is given, much is received. You are the one going to Bible school and gaining knowledge of my word. You know better, so do better."

That encounter with God caused me to see myself. I realized pride was sitting on the throne of my heart and not God. It was hard for me to deny myself and put someone else first, but I had to be honest with God and asked him to take away the anger, the hurt, the pride, and the pain of my heart and help me to have compassion and be more like him. I realize I was not obeying my husband and God was not pleased with my behavior. Thank God for my deliverance, and he is still working on me. Praise God! I have learned to love my husband in a new way and thank God for him because he was not the root of my problem; pride was. Sometimes we blame others instead of looking into the mirror, seeing ourselves, and being honest with ourselves and with God. When God reached out to Adam because of his disobedience instead of Adam being honest with God and repenting of what he had done, he blamed Eve, and it cost him his fellowship with God. (Read Genesis 3 KJV.)

Prayer

Heavenly Father, I pray in the name of Jesus that you would help us to be honest with you, especially in prayer. God, nothing is hidden from you, so help us to understand that when we are honest with you, it helps us to walk in true deliverance. Father, we know that you want to commune with us, so God gives us the strength to get up out of our bed and seek you earnestly in the morning. In Jesus's name, amen.

Waiting in Prayer

Waiting is a part of life experience that most people wish they could avoid. For example, people wait in traffic, at the doctor's office, or at the post office picking up packages. However, waiting is one method God uses to get our attention because when things do not work out the way we intend, we are forced to wait on the Lord. Waiting reminds us that we are not in control of our lives, but God is, and waiting on the Lord builds our confidence in him. In Genesis 12:1–2 (KJV), the Lord says to Abram, "Go from your country, your people and your father's household to the land I will show you. I will make you into a great nation, and I will bless you; I will make your name great, and you will be a blessing. I will bless those who bless you, and whoever curses you I will curse, and all peoples on earth will be blessed through you."

> Now, Sarai, Abram's wife, had not been able to bear children for him, but she had an Egyptian servant named Hagar. So Sarai said to Abram, "The Lord has prevented me from having children. Go and sleep with my servant. Perhaps I can have children through her." Abram agreed to Sarai's proposal, so Sarai, Abram's wife, took Hagar, her Egyptian servant, and gave her to Abram as a wife. (This happened ten years after Abram had settled in the land of Canaan.) Abram had sexual relations with Hagar, and she became pregnant. However, once Hagar discovered that she was pregnant, she began to treat her mistress, Sarai, with contempt. (Genesis 16:1–4 NLT)

Notice that when God first spoke to Abram, he was childless, but God told him that he was going to make him a great nation. After several years of waiting, we can assume that Sarai became impatient waiting on God, so she decided to help God out by telling her husband that she had a phenomenal idea about how to bring a child into the world because God was taking too long. During those times, when women were not able to conceive, they would give their handmaids to their husbands (read Genesis 30). The scripture indicates that Sarai doubted God and thought it was ridiculous for her to have a baby because she had passed the age of childbearing, so she told Abram to take her handmaid, Hagar.

Some of us are like Sarah thinking we can help God out. But God does not need our help or advice because he's in control and may I remind you that he knows what he's doing. So, when we are praying it's not for us to tell him what to do but to petition him and wait patiently for his answer.

What many of us don't understand is that we are in the classroom called life taking the class called waiting. We can pass the class by waiting for God's specific instructions on what to do, or we can go through every season planning our next move without consulting him and never move up to the next level, where waiting becomes a little more comfortable. We may be able to escape accidents and cheat death, but we cannot escape the waiting period each of us has to go through. Not waiting on God can cause you to make the wrong decision, which will eventually cause you to have added drama in your life. Do not let waiting on God negate the miracles he has for you. Give the miracle time to manifest while you wait. Had Sarai and Abram waited for God, their family drama with Hagar could have been avoided.

There are benefits to waiting in prayer. First of all, waiting on God gives you strength during any circumstance, so when you are faced with a dilemma, there is no need for anxiety. "Wait on the Lord: be of good courage, and he shall strengthen thine heart: wait, I say, on the Lord" (Psalm 27:14 KJV).

If you spend more time waiting on the Lord than rushing to do things your way, your life experience will be so much better, and you will experience a greater level of deliverance in your walk with him. Today, the majority of us think life passes at a fast pace, but we should not let this world's activities condition our lives. Part of our prayer time should be geared toward waiting to hear what the Lord wants to say and how he will lead us in our daily routines. Waiting is one of the elements of prayer that must be practiced. "The LORD is good to those who wait for him, to the soul who seeks him" (Lamentations 3:25 KJV).

The more we wait on God in prayer, the less impatient we will become with other people around us because while we are waiting on God, he is working things out. Waiting on God is a form of prayer because we should not only talk to God, but we must also wait for him to respond. "Therefore, the LORD waits to be gracious to you, and therefore he exalts himself to show mercy to you. For the LORD is a God of justice; blessed are all those who wait for him" (Isaiah 30:18 KJV).

Prayer cannot just be a one-way conversation. Just because Jesus commands us to pray to our heavenly Father doesn't mean we should not wait for his voice to respond. "But as for me, I will look to the Lord; I will wait for the God of my salvation; my God will hear me" (Micah 7:7 KJV).

One way to know that your prayer is answered is by waiting and getting the witness in your spirit. I am not saying that if you do not wait for the answer, God will not answer; all I want you to see is that when you wait for the confirmation of God, the enemy cannot play tricks on your mind throughout the day by telling you that your prayer was in vain and God was not listening. Sometimes the enemy will bring up your past by trying to convince you that what you did canceled out the answer. But if you wait to hear God's voice or if you get that sense of peace, you can remind the enemy that the prayer is already answered because God promised he would hear us when we pray.

> And we are confident that he hears us whenever we ask for anything that pleases him. And, since we know He hears us when we make our requests, we also know that He will give us what we ask for. (1 John 5:14–15 NLT)

Second, waiting releases the promise of the Holy Ghost. The disciples were given instructions to wait for the promise. After Jesus's suffering, he presented himself to them and gave many convincing proofs that he was alive. He appeared to them over a period of forty days and spoke about the kingdom of God. On one occasion, while he was eating with them, he gave them this command: "Do not leave Jerusalem but wait for the gift my Father promised, which you have heard me speak about. For John truly baptized you with water, but he shall be baptized with the Holy Ghost not many days hence" (Acts 1:3–5 KJV).

Can you imagine if the disciples had not waited in prayer and been in agreement with one another in the upper room? The Holy Ghost would have been delayed, and the three thousand souls that were saved on Pentecost probably would not have been. There is no way we can lead a successful life without the Holy Ghost, so during our prayer time, we need to yield, wait in his presence, and allow him to be immersed in us for the use of his kingdom on earth. Waiting brings the word that God promises for you into manifestation. So, choose to wait on God; after all, he is the one in control, not you.

Third, waiting brings peace and causes you to be focused and not rush to decide in haste.

> I will climb my watchtower now and wait to see what answer. And the Lord said to me, "Write my answer on a billboard, large and clear, so that anyone can read it at a glance and rush to tell the others. But these things I plan won't happen right away. Slowly, steadily, surely, the time approaches when the vision will be fulfilled. If it seems slow, do not despair, for these things will surely come to pass. Just be patient! They will not be overdue a single day!" (Habakkuk 2:2–4 TLB)

God has given you visions and dreams, and my encouragement to you is to wait on it. Waiting does not mean that you sit in one spot and expect it to happen. Waiting on God means you trust he knows what he's doing, and you wait for it to come to pass while you carry on with your life. So many of us regret things because we did not have the patience to wait. But we don't have to keep dwelling on the failures; we can decide from this day forward that we are going to be patient by waiting on God. The only way to conquer waiting is by waiting. The enemy does not have the faintest idea about your future; he just knows that there is greatness in your future. So, be patient and wait. God is obligated to provide for you if you are his child, so wait on God's promises to you to be fulfilled.

Prayer

Father, I pray that you will help me to wait on you. Give me the wisdom to know that your timing is best. Help me to be like Job, who decided to wait until his change came. Waiting is not easy, Father, but help me to trust your ways, in Jesus's name.

Be Guilty of Prayer

Even though prayer works, it is hard to imagine the reason some Christians do not pray to God daily. If Christians are going to be guilty of something other than holy living, it should be for prayer. Prayer is our lifeline that keeps us connected to God the Father. One of the most valuable assets we have in prayer is the name of Jesus, so it is vital to seal our prayers in his name. If you are not praying in the name of Jesus, you are praying beneath your privilege.

Daniel, one of the major prophets in the New Testament, stayed busy because he had a prayer relationship with his God. He was a young man who was taken out of his comfort zone, a place where he was loved and was taught the word of God. Although Daniel was no longer with his family, he still upheld the law of his ancestors. He practiced a religious principle that all Christians should model today.

The Bible says that Daniel prayed three times a day, and because of his prayer life, he had favor with God and was able to operate in a spirit of excellence. Daniel had a glimpse of the future where his life was characterized by faith, prayer, and consistency. He dared to stand on the word of God and refused to compromise. Because of his holy standard and prayer life, it's my understanding that it caused him to become the third ruler of the Babylonian kingdom. By being in charge of the governors and because of his moral principles, Daniel was the envy of government officials. He was brought up on charges because of his integrity. At an early age, Daniel had been taught to uphold the law and the principles of God's word. Although he was in a strange land, a place where people worshiped idols, the truth was embedded in his heart from a young age. So, despite the challenges, Daniel continued to serve his God even in his older years. Meanwhile, Daniel's accusers, the president, and the princes could not find anything to accuse him of. So, they conspired against him and went to the king to put a new law into effect: no one should pray to any god for thirty days. Doing so would result in capital punishment. Thus, when he found out about his attackers' accusations against him, because of his prayer life, Daniel did what he did best: he continued to pray because he had been taught to look to the temple if carried away in a strange land. (Read 1 Kings 8:44–54.)

People are not going to agree with you when you stand for the truth, especially in a heathen territory, because they do not understand your relationship with your God. God will cause you to stand out, and it will have nothing to do with you personally but for his glory. He wants to showcase you, and his display of you could be put on the radar of the enemy. Job 1:6–8 KJV says,

> One day the angels came to present themselves before the LORD, and Satan also came with them. The LORD said to Satan, "Where have you come from?" Satan answered the LORD, "From roaming throughout the earth, going back and forth on it." Then the LORD said to Satan, "Have you considered my servant Job? There is no one on earth like him; he is blameless and upright, a man who fears God and shuns evil."

God literally told the enemy to test Job because he knew Job would keep his end of the bargain by trusting God.

Are you in a position for God to boast about you? Daniel was destined to be great, and because of his potential, he was on the devil's hit list. But that did not stop him from serving his God or cause him to cancel a prayer meeting with God.

The scripture says, "Now when Daniel knew that the writing was signed, he went into his house; and his windows being open in his chamber toward Jerusalem, he kneeled upon his knees three times a day, and prayed, and gave thanks before his God, as he did aforetime" (Daniel 6:10 KJV). Clearly, Daniel did not allow the decree to stop him from performing his normal prayer routine. He continued to pray. I believe that somehow Daniel knew that we are to "pray without ceasing." Prayer was not an option; it was a command. And he was not going to let the charges discourage him from praying. Talking to God was the norm for him, so getting bad news was not going to take him off his regular course. Daniel showed no signs of anxiety. He was not acting out of character. He demonstrated that he knew God personally. Perhaps in his prayer time he prayed, "God, this situation is under your control. I don't know how you are going to come through, but I know you will."

When prayer is a part of your lifestyle, you do not change it because of unfavorable circumstances. In fact, you should continue as if it were a normal day. I know something will cause our emotions to be unstable, some problem will even shake us to our foundation, but prayer will keep us on track. If we trust God in hardship, pray, and give God space to work, he will manifest his glory. The interesting twist about this chapter is the fact that the king recognized Daniel's God as a mighty God. Notice what the king says to Daniel: "May your God whom you serve

> When prayer is a part of your lifestyle, you do not change it because of unfavorable circumstances.

continually save you" (Daniel 6:20 KJV). In other words, may your God whom you not only boast about but pray to every day deliver you. The king believed that Daniel's God would have to save him because when a king issues a decree, it cannot be changed. Not only did the king issue a decree, but he also spoke faith on Daniel's behalf. Psalm 34:19 KJV says, "Many are the afflictions of the righteous: but the LORD delivereth him out of them all." God will not allow our enemies to win us over. Surprisingly, the heathen king who had issued the decree humbled himself before God because he knew there was something different about Daniel. King Darius was looking for a way to protect Daniel, so he chose to follow one of Daniel's methods—fasting—as a spiritual discipline, which could be practiced at any given time. (Detailed information about fasting will be given in chapter 3.)

Daniel was found guilty of praying and was thrown into the lion's den because he chose to obey the command of God. Ironically, prayer as well as living to please God can put us in a difficult situation at times, but in the end, God will deliver us because he is able to. We cannot be afraid of facing trials. Jesus says, "In this life we shall have tribulation but be of good courage" (John 16:33 KJV). In Daniel's case, we see God coming through. Daniel was able to overcome his situation because prayer was part of his daily routine, so in his times of difficulty, he knew who his source was, and he knew that his strength was in prayer. The outcomes of Daniel's deliverance are a result of the fact that he prayed. Daniel's prayers propelled him to the next dimension of his life. He was promoted. If we fail to pray, we have fallen into the group of the not guilty, and in this phase of life, we need to be guilty of praying. When we are guilty of praying, we open the door for God to intervene on behalf of the ones we love.

Sophia L. Garcia

Personal Testimony

I must admit that I am guilty of not praying enough. I know God is expecting me to surrender my all to him and pray not when it's convenient but to follow his command and pray always. It is not impossible to pray anytime because we do not need to be in building to pray; we just need to have a praying spirit and be sensitive to the Holy Ghost.

Prayer

Oh Lord, guide us so we can become more aware of your presence in spite of our situation. Help us to be faithful to you in prayer, knowing that you will give us the victory in Jesus's name, amen.

3

Power of Prayer

Prayer is not so much about the word we utter to God but rather the motives of our hearts.

Even though prayer is no longer the impelling force of many churches, it is imperative that we pray because the enemy wants to impede our entry to the throne room. The more we visit the throne room of God, the easier it is for us to converse with him. The power of the prayer does not hinge so much on the words we use but to whom we pray and what we pray for. "Ask, and it shall be given you; seek, and you shall find; knock, and it shall be opened to you" (Matthew 7:7 KJV). "If he abide in me and my word abide in you, he shall ask what he will, and it shall be done unto you" (John 15:7 KJV). Those are powerful scriptures, but we will not see the manifestation of it in our life without faith. Yes, there are limitations to prayers, but to have power in prayer, we must be obedient to God's word, and we must submit our spirit to

> *It is imperative that we pray because the enemy wants to impede our entry to the throne room.*

his will. The power of prayer teaches you how to discern the will of the Spirit of God. If you are a child of God, you can no longer just read the word of God only to gain knowledge, but you must also embrace the Spirit of God to do his due diligence.

We are in an era when God wants to pour out his Spirit upon all flesh, and we must position ourselves to change the atmosphere and to usher in the glory of God. It can no longer be the church as usual, where the body of Christ comes together Sunday after Sunday for a social gathering. The church was never designed for social gatherings. The church is a vehicle to transport the people of God to a greater understanding of who God is.

> How, then, can people call on one they do not believe in? And how can they believe in one whom they have not heard? And how can they hear without someone preaching to them? (Romans 10:14 KJV)

The power of prayer is in the strength and unity of the believers. God desires unity among his believers so they can operate as one body. In the book of beginning (Genesis 11 KJV), at the Tower of Babel, the people were in such unity that God changed their language and separated them so they would not be able to fulfill their dreams of getting to heaven and making a name for themselves. Even though their motives were misguided, God has designed humankind to get to heaven. The bottom line is those people were operating under the same principles with one another. They were in accord with one another. When believers agree with God, he will do wonders among his people.

> *To gain power in prayer, one must have the attention of God's ears and say what God's word say.*

To gain power in prayer, one must have the attention of God's ears and say what

God's words say. The word cannot return to him void, but it shall accomplish what we sent it forth to do. Jesus is the word (John 1), so when you are praying, just picture Jesus's hands at work, and there will be no way he can go to his father and say, "Daddy, I could not carry out that task that you assigned me to do." God's word assures us that he will release the answer when we pray. "I will answer them before they even call to me. While they are still talking about their needs, I will go ahead and answer their prayers!" (Isaiah 65:24 NLT). When the church prays, we are sending a message to the enemy to let him know that we know who the commander-in-chief is, who is in control, and who oversees every aspect of our lives.

> Now about that time Herod the king stretched forth his hands to vex certain of the church. And he killed James the brother of John with the sword. And because he saw it pleased the Jews, he proceeded further to take Peter also. (Then were the days of unleavened bread.) And when he had apprehended him, he put him in prison, and delivered him to four quaternions of soldiers to keep him; intending after Easter to bring him forth to the people. Peter therefore was kept in prison: but prayer was made without ceasing of the church unto God for him. And when Herod would have brought him forth, the same night Peter was sleeping between two soldiers, bound with two chains: and the keepers before the door kept the prison. And, behold, the angel of the Lord came upon him, and a light shined in the prison: and he smote Peter on the side, and raised him up, saying, Arise up quickly. And his

chains fell off from his hands. And the angel said unto him, Gird thyself, and bind on thy sandals. And so he did. And he saith unto him, Cast thy garment about thee, and follow me. And he went out, and followed him; and wist not that it was true which was done by the angel; but thought he saw a vision. (Acts 12:1–9 KJV)

Luke tells us that the church was in conflict with King Herod, who had James killed. James was the brother of John, and because it pleased the Jews, Herod got Peter arrested. Just because the devil won one victory in our lives doesn't mean he's on a winning streak. In 2016 the Cleveland (Cavs) came back from a 3–1 victory—something that was never done in the history of the NBA—beating the Golden State Warriors. The Warriors fans thought it would be a sweep, but somehow the Cavaliers find the strength and use the strategy they know in basketball to make history.

The power of prayer is like dribbling the basketball from the half court and shooting a slam dunk in the enemy's face. If you know someone who has been accused of a crime and is incarcerated, you may not be able to go beyond the prison walls, but you can send a prayer and allow the Holy Spirit to take control. When Peter was locked up in prison during the Passover, he was put under maximum security because of his reputation. One could only assume that he had no visiting rights, and the rest of the apostles were probably afraid to visit because their association with Peter could have made them the next target for a life sentence. However, they did not allow

> The power of prayer is like dribbling the basketball from the half court and shooting a slam dunk in the enemy's face.

that to discourage them from praying. They called a prayer meeting, and their prayers invaded God's space and got his attention. The prayer was so intense, filled with faith and boldness, that God gave an angel the command to release Peter. I believe our heavenly Father had a meeting with the Godhead (triune God) and concluded that this type of prayer could not be left unanswered. His people depended on him, so he needed to rescue Peter. Peter's deliverance needed divine intervention; only an infinite God could have performed such a miracle. What an awesome experience that must have been for Peter! The scripture divulges that Peter was sleeping; he showed no sign of desperation. Peter was not worried about being in prison; he was not up all night trying to figure out the turbulence he was going through. Maybe before he went to sleep, he had whispered a prayer, saying, "Lord, I don't know how this is going to turn out, but I know you can work it out." Or perhaps in the moment when he was captured, the words of Jesus echoed in his heart: "Peace I leave with you; my peace I give unto you; not as the world giveth, give I unto you. Let not your heart be troubled, neither let it be afraid" (John 14:27 KJV).

After the angel released Peter from prison, he went to the house where the saints gathered to pray for him, and when he knocked on the door, they did not believe it was him because of the quick miracle God had performed. You may not be in an actual prison, but it sure can feel like you are in bondage because of the intense pressure. To escape this, you should have an audience with God. The power of prayer can penetrate the atmosphere of your surroundings and command the shackles to break and the chains to disappear. As I stated earlier, it took divine intervention on Peter's behalf. God is no "respecter of person." *He is the same yesterday, today, and forever,* and angels are waiting to hear the command of God to do battle on his children's behalf, so keep on praying because God can immediately work on your behalf. When we think of miracles, sometimes our conclusion is this is difficult to do, and it puts our minds in a place of desperation. But the next time you need a miracle, pray and believe that this is something God is able to do.

Personal Testimony

I remember one day when I was praying; the scripture came to me, "Do two walk together unless they have agreed to do so?" (Amos 3:3 NIV).

I said, "Yes, I understand. I cannot walk with someone who does not believe the same things I do."

I heard a voice saying I wasn't talking about your fellowship with other people. He was talking about my agreeing with him and his word. I was praying but not believing that what I was praying for would actually come to pass. I had to ask him to help me with my unbelief.

Many of us do not believe that what we are praying for will come to pass. And sometimes we do not believe we are the ones God wants to bless because of what we have done in the past. But the blood of Jesus gives us a clean record. God does not hold our past against our future. So, keep on praying because our prayers will produce the strength we need to believe God for miracles.

Prayer

Father, help me to believe what I prayed for will come to fruition. There are no limits to what you can do. Help my unbelief in Jesus's name. Amen!

The Power of the Spoken Word

The power of the spoken word is being able to believe God regardless of what's going on in our world. Words are powerful. Just one word can cause your life to be impacted. Words have the power to heal or to break one's spirit. The scripture declares, "We can decree a thing and it shall be established unto thee" (Job 22:28 KJV). We cannot focus our energy on what's going on in society and be so distracted that we forget that we have power in our voice to change things. Saying what God says requires confidence in him and his word. For our faith to be built up, we must continuously pray and read the word of God. By reading the word, we will see the experiences of people who serve God and have emerged victorious from the storms of life. Acts 27 gives us the understanding that Paul spoke the word during a storm and declared no life would be lost because of the storm, and everyone made it to shore because of the spoken word.

> The power of the spoken word is being able to believe God regardless of what's going on in our world.

The Bible provides a clear understanding of Acts 3 that Peter and John went to the temple together for prayer. Before they went to the temple, there was a lame man at the gate called Beautiful. I believe it was God's intent for the lame man to be healed. Peter and John were on an assignment that day. When it is your time for a breakthrough, God will orchestrate your miracle. The scripture says this man was carried to the temple every day, perhaps Peter and John were caught up in their assignment in the church, so they walked into the temple without giving the beggar any attention. But on this day, the Holy Ghost prompted them to notice the man in his condition. They had to put rituals and traditions asides. For a moment they realized they had to focus on someone else's needs. Notice they said to the beggar that they did not have silver and gold, but what they had, they would give to him, so in the name of Jesus, he should rise and walk. In other words, they did not have the temporary blessings that the beggar was asking for, but they had the power of the spoken word that would allow him to function as an average person. Therefore, Christians cannot be so caught up in religious activities that we have no time for people with disabilities.

For years, this man hung out at the house of prayer, but prayer was not offered. Thank God for the spoken word.

Judging from a human perspective, I do not think the man was expecting his life to be impacted. He was expecting something tangible. But the spoken word caused his feet and ankle bones to receive strength so he would no longer need to be carried to the temple. He could walk freely and go to the temple to praise God. This man's life was changed because of the spoken word. Is there a word in your mouth that needs to be spoken on behalf of someone today? God has given us opportunities each day to encourage someone. So, instead of speaking words that can wound someone and scare him or her for life, use your words carefully today.

The power of the spoken word has power to activate or to create things. Luke gives us an explicit reference to the conversation Jesus had with Peter of how powerful the spoken word is in 5:4–8 (KJV). Jesus gave Peter simple instructions by sending him back into the water to fish.

> Now when he had left speaking, he said unto Simon, launch out into the deep, and let down your nets for a draught. And Simon answering said unto him,

Master, we have toiled all the night, and have taken nothing: nevertheless, at thy word, I will let down the net. And when they had this done, they inclosed a great multitude of fishes: and their net brake. And they beckoned unto their partners, which were in the other ship, that they should come and help them. And they came and filled both the ships, so that they began to sink. When Simon Peter saw it, he fell down at Jesus' knees, saying, Depart from me; for I am a sinful man, O LORD.

Jesus told Peter to go back into the deep, but Peter was discouraged because he had been fishing all night and did not catch any fish. His response to Jesus shows that he was annoyed because Jesus should have understood that fishing was his lifestyle and that he was not a novice at fishing; it was something he had been doing before he had met Jesus. He took Jesus at his spoken word and acted on obedience, not faith, because he did not believe there were fishes for him to catch, but he obeyed the voice of Jesus, and because of his willingness, he caught more fish than he could handle. This emphasis caused him to experience the overflow. God wants us to experience abundance. If we are not obedient to his spoken word, we hinder our blessing. Sometimes God will allow things not to go the way we plan them on purpose so he can speak a word that seems contrary to where he wants to take us, but it's up to us to trust him and wait for the result. When we read the book of Exodus, we saw where God commissioned Moses to go to Egypt and tell Pharaoh to let his people go. Nonetheless, God then turned around and hardened Pharaoh's heart. After several attempts, Moses' impulsive request caused him to see God's magnificent power in action.

Our faith should not depend on human efforts but rather the miracle-working power of God. When we allow faith to take preeminence in our lives, God is well pleased. We cannot go to God with a doubtful mind and expect him to dispatch an angel to work on our behalf. We must be God's mouthpiece on earth, and we must give him something to work with because faith is the entrance to the heart of God that allows prayer to dominate the earth. This is what Elijah the prophet did when he stood in the reign of Ahab, the ungodly king who turned the heart of the people to idolatry, and said it would not rain according to his words. Notice that the prophet did not mention that the word of the Lord declared it, nor did he say that it was according to the word of the Lord. What Elijah did was put his faith into action; his unwavering faith caused God to shut the heavens for a period, and it did not rain. Isaiah 65:24 (NLT) says, "I will answer them before they even call to me. While they are still talking about their needs, I will go ahead and answer their prayers!" The prophet did not even consider his life and how he would also be affected. Because of his faith, God made provisions for him and told him to go to Mount Carmel, where he was going to feed him. He just knew that God would be able to do this because God had allowed it to rain for forty nights and days during Noah's era. The same God who causes it to rain can stop it from raining, so he spoke in faith, believing that God was going to support him. And it did not rain on the earth for three and a half years, according to the scripture. What great faith Elijah the prophet

> What Elijah did was put his faith into action. His unwavering faith caused God to shut the heavens for a period, and it did not rain.

possessed. The scripture shows no evidence that he was filled with the Holy Ghost, but he had an understanding of who God was and the power he possesses. Elijah was not immortal; he was a human being just like us. The only difference between him and most of us is that he chose to believe in God. If God is going to do miracles in our lives, we have to believe him. And the more we believe him, the greater the opportunity for him to "move us from faith to faith." Faith cannot be exhausted, and there are no boundaries to what the power of the spoken word will allow us to carry out as God's assignment on earth. There will be times when we may not be able to see God's hands at work, but faith will propel us to believe in him.

Joshua, the son of Nun, is another great example of the spoken word. God spoke to Joshua during his early stage in the ministry, telling him that he would be with him, and no man shall be able to stand before him, and he was not going to let him down (paraphrasing). When the Amorites were too much for Joshua to handle, he remembered the word of God. If you ever find yourself in a place where it seems as if nothing is coming together and you have an urgency to quit the faith, instead of complaining, speak of faith, and give God some room to work. Joshua asked the Lord to give the Israelites victory over the Amorites. He prayed to the Lord in front of all the people of Israel. He said, "Let the sun stand still over Gideon and the moon over the valley of Aijalon." So the sun and moon stood still until the Israelites had defeated their enemies. The sun stopped in the middle of the sky, and it did not set as on a normal day. (Joshua 10:1-13)

The fact of the calendar is that nearly every four years, we add an extra day to the calendar in the form of February 29, which is also known as leap day. www.timeanddate.com stated that: Leap years are needed to keep our modern-day Gregorian calendar in alignment with the earth's revolutions around the sun. It takes the earth approximately 365.242189 days—or 365 days, 5 hours, 48 minutes, and 45 seconds—to circle once around the sun. This is called a tropical year and is measured from the March equinox. However, the Gregorian calendar has only 365 days in a year, so if we didn't add a leap day on February 29 every four years, we would lose almost six hours off our calendar every year. After only 100 years, our calendar would be off by around 24 days! (November 2017)

The fact that scientists recognized that the earth is out of rotation indicated that divine intervention won Joshua battle. I am a firm believer that this happened because Joshua maximized his potential by exercising his faith and calling the sun to stand still.

Personal Testimony

Before my oldest son, David was born, the doctors were preparing me for the worst-case scenario. While they were talking to me, I had a praying spirit. So, when they were telling me that the baby's lungs were not developed and that it was possible the baby would not live, a voice spoke to me and said, "If I can blow breath into Adam and Eve, this child will come out breathing." So, I turned to the doctors and screamed for everyone to shut up. They looked at me as if I were crazy. A few hours later, when I gave birth to my son, I knew something was wrong right away because of the look on the doctor's face. A few minutes later, I found out that I was supposed to be dead because of a ruptured placenta the day before I delivered. I knew only God could have worked that miracle, and I truly believe somebody was praying for me.

After I had come out of recovery, a nurse came to my room to tell me that my premature baby was in the intensive care unit and that he would be in the hospital for a couple of months. My response was the spoken word that my child would be in the ICU for a couple of days only. The nurse said, "Ma'am, your baby is in the ICU, and he will be here for a couple of months." I told her my child was in the ICU, but he would be there for only a couple of days. After the nurse's third attempt to convince me, she left the room because I had chosen to believe God and spoke faith into action. Within three days, my child was released to go home from the ICU. Months later, I realized I had responded once for the Father, once for the Son, and once for the Holy Ghost.

My son was diagnosed with asthma. I was given a breathing machine to use at home if he had an asthma attack and an inhaler to use on a regular basis. During his first three years, he was a regular patient at the Beth Israel emergency department. One night, David had an asthma attack, and I told my brother to start the car while I got him ready. However, I refused to accept this was the way my son would live for the rest of his life. So, I told my brother Owen to shut off the car because Bishop Stacey McQueen said to me at my daughter's homegoing service in 1997 that God would bless me with healthy children, and I held God to that promise. Therefore, I took David, held him up to God, and said, "You promised me a healthy child," and seventeen years later, he has not had another asthma attack.

If God gives you his word, hold on to that word and pray over the promises of God because "God is not a man, so he does not lie. He is not human, so he does not change his mind. Has he ever spoken and failed to act? Has he ever promised and not carried it through?" (Numbers 23:19 NLT).

Prayer

Father, in the name of Jesus, I bind the spirit of fear and release faith now to my brother/sister who's reading this book. Let him/her know that what you promise shall come to pass and that it's never too late to remind you of your word that was spoken in Jesus's name. Amen!

Secret Weapon—Fasting

We can pray without fasting, but we cannot fast without praying to get supernatural result!

Fasting is taking the focus off of yourself and putting your attention on God. It's the afflicting of one's soul. It is one of the most powerful spiritual weapons that believers have, and I believe it is the least used among the people of God. "Sanctify ye a fast, call a solemn assembly, gather the elders and all the inhabitants of the land into the house of the Lord your God, and cry" (Joel 1:14 KJV).

The Old Testament scriptures indicate that it is God's intent for all believers to fast because fasting restores our relationship with him. The New Testament scriptures make it clear that Jesus is not asking us to fast; he's expecting us to do so:

> When you fast, do not look somber as the hypocrites do, for they disfigure their faces to show others they are fasting. Truly I tell you, they have received their reward in full. But when you fast, put oil on your head and wash your face, so that it will not be obvious to others that you are fasting, but only to your Father, who is unseen; and your Father,

who sees what is done in secret, will reward you. (Matthew 6:16–18 NIV)

Jesus also said, "If any man come after me let him first deny himself and take up your cross and follow me" (Mark 8:34 KJV).

Life can sometimes get hectic and cause us to lose our spiritual awareness, and we become mediocre. Instead of serving God out of reverence, we operate on empty and serve God out of activities. Fasting will move us away from the mundane and help us to navigate our way back to a place of spiritual awakening that brings both reward and result. It is a spiritual discipline that needs to be practiced by all born-again believers unless they have a medical condition that restricts them. When we as believers live our lives without fasting, the secret weapon, we may not be aware that we are giving the enemy a spare key to our spirit. And when Satan sees the opportunity to open the door for us to operate in our flesh, he doesn't mind using that key. We cannot afford to give the enemy permission to our spirit, so periodically we must fast. Fasting not only shuts down the voice of the enemy but also helps us combat the plan of the enemy. The enemy wants to annihilate the plan of God for our lives; that's why he does not want us to fast.

Notice that when you intend to go on a fast, your body starts to experience all types of changes, such as nausea, headache, and even weakness. This kind of change is usually because our flesh wants to be in control, but we cannot allow our flesh to dictate to us what we should do when it comes to fasting and bettering our relationship with the Lord. Fasting not only helps us spiritually, but it also helps detoxify our bodies and cleanse us from toxic buildup. Before going on a fast, start drinking a lot of water, cut down on junk food as well as beverages high in caffeine, and start eating healthy. This will help you cope during the fast. Your mind is going to tell you it's not going to work; you can't do this. But Christians need to adopt the biblical principles of fasting. The Bible describes three main forms of fasting: (1) normal fast, involving total abstinence from food but not from water (Luke 4:2); (2) abstinence from both food and water for no more than three days (Ezra 10:; Esther 4:16; Acts 9:9); and (3) restriction of diet rather than complete abstinence (Daniel 10:3; excerpt is taken from *Holman Concise Bible Dictionary*, pg. 236, C. Robert Marsh)

The US Army spends billions of dollars each year to make sure their weapons are updated, and soldiers are equipped with specialized equipment just in case another country wants to go to war or prey on innocent men, women, and children. No soldier wants to go to war unprepared. If the natural man has the wisdom to know how to become fully engaged in his preparations to protect the innocent, how much more so the children of God. They need to be prepared for spiritual battle. Fasting releases, the power of God and gives you access to uncharted territory and to rebuke, in the name of Jesus, witches and anyone who is possessed by demons.

> If the natural man has the wisdom to know how to become fully engaged in his preparations to protect the innocent, how much more so the children of God.

Demons are fallen angels. If you are not fasting, stay away from the demonic atmosphere. If you are someone who doesn't like to fast, please do not try to cast out demons—Satan's helpers—because they will embarrass you, just as they did the Jewish priest and the seven sons of Sceva. They were commanding evil spirits to get out of people using Paul's as well as Jesus's name. A man possessed by evil spirits jumped on them and started beating them, asking who gave them the authority to disturb them. The priest and the seven sons of Sceva ran out into the community without their clothes because they were no match for the evil spirit (Acts 19:13–15, paraphrased). They saw what Paul had done, not knowing that to have the power of Jesus takes more than just going to church functions. *We cannot have a form of godliness and deny the power of God* (paraphrasing 2 Peter 3:5 KJV).

You must spend time in prayer as well as fasting. If we are going to make an impact on the world, we must live lives of consecration. *Consecration* can simply refer to being separated or set apart for God's use because we don't know when a situation may present itself, and we must be to be ready to cast an evil spirit out. The priest and the sons of Sceva noticed that the evil spirit had answered them and said, "Paul and Jesus we know, but who are you?" It's not time to play church; it's time to be the church.

Matthew tells us that Jesus's disciples faced a similar situation when a father brought his son, who was demon possessed, and asked the disciples to heal him. Jesus's disciples were unsuccessful in healing the son (paraphrasing chapter 17: 21 KJV). The disciples were disappointed in the whole ordeal because they were not able to cast the demon out of the son without Jesus being in their presence. They had seen Jesus perform miracles before and could not understand why they were not able to do the same. Privately, they went to Jesus to ask why they could not cast the demon out of the child. Jesus told his disciples, "This kind come by fasting and praying." Also, Jesus brought it to their attention that doubt was the common factor that they all possess including the child's father which prevented the child's deliverance. When doubt and uncertainty are in operation; it cancels out a miracle. If believers are going to carry out the mission of God, we must have faith to believe; we cannot hesitate in our faith or be intimidated by unusual circumstances. This is why every child of God needs to make fasting a priority in his or her life—because fasting helps alleviate doubts. Sometimes we struggle with our faith but don't become disheartened. Just ask the master to increase your faith when you're fasting.

Fasting will humble your soul and keep your spirit aligned with God's will for your life. When you are on a fast, it's not for you to boast and announce to everyone you encounter. I believe there are things people can do to increase their spiritual capacity when fasting, such as getting involved in prayer meetings as well as giving. You can increase your offerings by dropping extra in the offering box and giving to the less fortunate. However, it doesn't have to be something tangible; you can give your time by visiting the sick or shut-ins or visiting the elderly, spending quality time with them by reading to them, or listening to their stories from the past. This will open the door of opportunity for God to reward you. He will reward you by increasing your prayer life, manifesting his presence in your life, or giving you insight into his word. We cannot be on a fast and go through the routine of everyday activities.

> Wherefore have we fasted, say they, and thou seest not? Wherefore have we afflicted our soul, and thou takest no knowledge? Behold, on the day of your fast ye find pleasure, and exact all your labors. (Isaiah 58:3 KJV)

We must discipline ourselves by shutting down the desire of our flesh; restrict ourselves from television and social media except for work-related business; and limit our phone conversations with friends by putting away empty gestures.

Fasting is not just skipping a meal for the day. You must also have the right attitude because when you are fasting, your spirit is vulnerable, and whatever you feed your spirit will be the result of the fast. For example, if you are fasting and all you do that day is complain about what has gone wrong in your life when the fast is over, you will inherit a spirit of complaining. If you choose to pray and believe in God, your faith will increase. Also, we have to remember that when the period of fasting is over, we must break our fast with prayer, even if it's five minutes, and not be so quick to rush back to bad habits, such as watching excessive television, because that would defeat the purpose of the fast. When fasting, read the word of God more frequently and pray with purpose. Tell God what you are fasting for and what you expect him to do, not just in your life but for any individual who needs a breakthrough. When you complement your fasting with prayer, you invoke the presence of God to be manifested in your life, and you will get supernatural results.

> After this, the Moabites and Ammonites with some of the Meunites came to wage war against Jehoshaphat. Some people came and told Jehoshaphat, "A vast army is coming against you from Edom, from the other side of the Dead Sea. It is already in Hazezon Tamar" (that is, En Gedi). Alarmed, Jehoshaphat resolved to inquire of the LORD, and he proclaimed a fast for all Judah. The people of Judah came together to seek help from the LORD; indeed, they came from every town in Judah to seek him. Then upon Jahaziel the son of Zechariah, the son of Benaiah, the son of Jeiel, the son of Mattaniah, a Levite of the sons of

Asaph, came the Spirit of the LORD in the midst of the congregation; And he said, hearken ye, all Judah, and ye inhabitants of Jerusalem, and thou king Jehoshaphat, Thus saith the LORD unto you, Be not afraid nor dismayed by reason of this great multitude; for the battle is not yours, but God's. To morrow go ye down against them: behold, they come up by the cliff of Ziz; and ye shall find them at the end of the brook, before the wilderness of Jeruel. Ye shall not need to fight in this battle: set yourselves, stand ye still, and see the salvation of the LORD with you, O Judah and Jerusalem: fear not, nor be dismayed; to morrow go out against them: for the LORD will be with you. which he did. (2 Chronicles 20:1-4,14-17 NKJV)

What a triumphant moment! The children of God fasted and produced results. They did not rely on their natural abilities or the army of Israel. To get a full understanding, read the whole chapter.

The book of Esther is another excellent example of God's divine intervention of deliverance as a result of fasting and prayer. Esther knew that she could not go before the king without permission because it was against the law for someone to go before the king without being requested into the king's chamber. She also knew there was no other way to save the Jewish nation, although Haman had a direct entrance to the ear-gate of the king. Esther had the opportunity to take a risk—a risk that would give her the attention of the king's heart. She knew it was risky, but her mind was made up to take the chance to go before the king because her uncle had already cautioned her that she might have come to this royal position for this time. So, Esther told the Jewish people to do an absolute fast with her for three days. After the fast was over, God gave her favor with the king to save her people from Haman, who had conspired against the Jews. Haman would have eradicated the Jewish nation if Esther had not had the courage to use her secret weapon. Bottom line, when the enemy sends threats, it may make us feel afraid, but if we would come together and fast, we would experience great deliverance from our extraordinary God. (Read the book of Ester)

Jesus fasted for forty days, which prepared him for ministry. He was able to overcome the lust of the flesh, the lust of the eyes, and the pride of life. (Read Matthew 4:4 KJV.) Fasting is not to be overlooked because it is the secret weapon believers can always use against the enemy to get God's attention.

Personal Testimony

I had a situation going on in my body, and because I was embarrassed and afraid to go to the doctor, I went on a fast. I told God I was expecting him to heal me. It so happened when I went to Sunday school, the topic was about faith. I started sharing my concerns and how I believed God. During the morning worship, after the pastor preached his sermon, he said, "There's a lady here with a condition in her body." I was in awe of God and was afraid to reveal myself until the pastor said, "She is sitting on the right side of the church." That's when I got up and started walking to the front of the church. While I was walking, the pastor said, "I don't have to lay hands; you are healed because of your faith." I knew it happened because I went on the fast, and God was able to heal my body.

Sophia L. Garcia

Prayer

Father, I pray that you will help us all to use the secret weapon of fasting so we can accomplish what you commissioned us to do. Oh God, I pray that you will help us to pray and read your word more, especially when fasting. These I ask in Jesus's name, amen!

4

INTERCESSORY PRAYER

And I sought for a man among them, that should make up the hedge, and stand in the gap before me for the land, that I should not destroy it: but I found none ... And he saw that there was no man, and wondered that there was no intercessor: therefore his arm brought salvation unto him; and his righteousness, it sustained him. (Ezekiel 22:30; Isaiah 59:16 KJV)

Could you be the one God is looking for to stand in the gap on this last and evil day? You may not have the gift of intercession, but that does not exclude you from interceding. Intercessory prayer is standing in the gap for someone else because you realize that someone else's needs may be greater than yours. If you are called to the ministry of prayer, be cognizant of the fact that at any moment, God can require your assistance for the person who is in need and be ready to engage in spiritual warfare. That means your sleep will be interrupted, and prayer is not always when you set a time, but it also includes the time when the Spirit prompts you to pray. I must admit that sometimes, it feels like a lonely path, and I wonder if I will be able to fit in with other people because God requires a daily surrendering of my will that causes me to act differently, so people think I am weird, but as lonely as the walk gets, my fulfillment and joy come when a prayer is answered on someone's behalf.

> As intercessors, God's will over our lives takes precedence over every other assignment, including preaching.

As intercessors, God's will over our lives takes precedence over every other assignment, including preaching. Yes, preaching! After wrestling with God for years, I finally got it. I knew I was called to pray but did not know prayer was the ministry God wanted me to birth because I also knew he called me to preach his word. I have seen a lot of preachers miss out on the awesome ministry God has called them to because they did not understand how to separate the ministry of prayer and the call to preach. I have been in services where the preacher would preach but did not have altar call, and neither did the preacher ask people to come together and pray. S/he will have finished preaching and then hand the microphone over and walk out of the services. Every intercessor is not called to preach, and every preacher is not called to intercede. But preachers are not exempt from praying. If God has given you the ability to pray and gifted you to preach, ask him to help you to understand which one is your first assignment. The most fulfilling moment is to know your purpose in life and to be able to operate in your assignment in the earth.

Generally speaking. If you are called to intercede and you are not praying for the people God put on your heart, it is like telling someone to run the red light during oncoming traffic. Intercessory prayer will help someone avoid roadblock in his or her life and put someone back on the right track. Intercessory prayers cause one to have discernment and to not only feel but also understand what people are going through in their lives. Therefore, discernment does not give us permission to be noisy in another person's business. But as an intercessor, you are in the learner driver's seat, waiting for instruction from the Holy Ghost because prayer is the driving force that will help you maneuver through the atmosphere for someone else's breakthrough.

> For the weapons of our warfare is not carnal, but It's mighty through God to the pulling down of strongholds; Casting down imaginations, and every high thing that exalteth itself against the knowledge of God, and bringing into captivity every thought to the obedience of Christ." (2 Corinthians 10:4–5 KJV)

Notice that the Bible uses the word *weapon*; this implies that we are at war, and at any given moment, our weapon must be put to good use. But this type of weapon is not a physical, material thing because our fight is not with a human being; our battle is spiritual, so we cannot use our fists to fight in this type of war. We must tackle this task using our weapon of prayer because the enemy is looking for a weak area in our lives to attack so he can change our mind about God. He wants us to doubt the word that God has given to us. But prayer is a mighty force in spiritual warfare. It does not matter what issues our family members are tied up in. In prayer, we can command the devil to let them lose by the power of the Holy Ghost. When you are interceding, you don't have to wonder if you are making an impact because you are doing one of the greatest ministries on the earth; you are in partnership with Christ. In fact, I believe no ministry can be effective without prayer, and your prayers will make a difference in the earth regardless of the circumstances. God is looking for someone he can trust who will make himself/ herself available for the prayer mantle. Intercessory prayer requires five key ingredients: repentance, consecration, discipline, the Holy Ghost, and love.

First of all, we cannot go into intercessory prayer without a repenting heart. "And when you stand praying, if you hold anything against anyone, forgive him, so that your Father in heaven may forgive you your sins" (Mark 11:25 KJV).

> Who may ascend the mountain of the LORD? Who may stand in his holy place? The one who has clean hands and a pure heart, who does not trust in an idol or swear by a false god. (Psalm 24:3–4 KJV)

Before we intercede for someone, our hands have to be clean, and it is imperative that we examine our hearts because we want to make sure there is no remnant from past experiences that dwells in our hearts. A clean hand is symbolic and ceremonial. (Read Leviticus 11.) This is why the Pharisees were perturbed when Jesus did not do the handwashing ceremony according to Jewish custom. (Read Luke 11:38.) Before a surgeon performs surgery, he has to wash his hands. Ironically, God told Moses in Exodus before the priest and Aaron went into the meeting place their hands had to be clean. (Read the full chapters Exodus 30:17–21, 40:30–32 KJV.) Symbolically, they were washing away anything that may have contaminated from their hands because the priest had to be holy going before a holy God. "In every place of worship, I want men to pray with holy hands lifted up to God, free from anger and controversy" (1 Timothy 2:8 NLT).

Also, nurses have to make sure all the instruments are sterilized and ready to be used for the next patient. It's necessary because there cannot be residues from the last operation. Not only the doctors will be at fault, but the hospital will also be liable because the person will be in the hands of the surgeon. If the instruments are not properly cleaned, the patient could be infected, which would create another problem that could be detrimental to the patient. So, before we start to intercede, we must make sure our hearts are right before God by asking God to search us. (Read Psalm 26:2). Sometimes we have done things to people that we are not aware of, so we have to ask God to forgive our sins of omission—the things we failed to do in our daily walk, for example, being nice to someone. We must also ask forgiveness for the sins of commission—the things that God commands us to do and we ignore when we don't do the things he commission us to do. We have to make sure to unload from our daily burdens and be serious about the people we are about to pray for because their breakthrough is in our hands. Someone might be in a life-or-death situation, and you have to bargain with God so he can grant life extension.

God was fed up with the sin of Sodom and Gomorrah because the sins of the people provoked him. Abraham stood in between God and the people, pleaded his case, and bargained with God. He said,

> Would you also destroy the righteous with the wicked? Suppose there were fifty righteous within the city; would you also desire the place and not spare it for the fifty righteous that were in it? Far it be from you to do such a thing as this, to slay the righteous

> with the wicked, so that the righteous should be as the wicked; for it be from you! Shall not the Judge of all the earth do right. (Genesis 18:23–24 NKJV)

God would have spared the city if he found at least ten righteous people. Unfortunately, there weren't enough righteous people to spare the city. Sad to say, the enemy is still fighting to take over the city. It is up to the children of God to take our rightful place and use the authority that God has given us. We have authority to bind and to lose. We can bind up principalities and power over our cities and loose the power of God to operate. We cannot afford for the enemy to parade through our cities as if God does not exist.

Second, is consecration. I dealt a little with consecration and the secret weapon—fasting—in chapter 3. Intercession requires a person to live a consecrated life, a life that is sold out to doing the Father's will. We must yield our minds, souls, and spirits to the Father, so the Spirit of God will pray through and for us. When people ask me to pray for them, I usually don't ask what the request is because I believe if God wants to reveal it, he will. Most times, he does that, which encourages me and proves to the person who is requesting the prayer that he is real. It is evidence that we serve a God who is all knowing. There is nothing wrong with asking people to tell you what their prayer request is or to let them share their concerns before praying because God will answer either way.

Consecration requires us to fast; you don't have to fast daily, but you must fast on a regular basis. Fasting causes you to reverence God with the spirit of humility and know that without him, you can do nothing, so you will not walk in the spirit of pride, thinking you are the one working the miracles instead of trusting in God's ability to answer your prayers.

With that mind-set, an intercessor is open to God and accepts his will if he chose not to answer our prayers that day. We understand that we need to be persistent, especially when praying for a loved one to experience salvation. Just because God didn't answer doesn't mean he cannot perform. The widow did not give up when the unjust judge told her the first no. She was persistent in her pursuit, believing that what she asked for would be granted. We must stand firm in our faith without wavering because James says,

> But let him asked in faith, nothing wavering. For he that wavereth is like the wave of the sea driven with the wind and tossed. For let not that man think he receive anything of the Lord. A double minded man is unstable in all his ways. (James 1:6-8 KJV)

Third, you need self-discipline to get the best result for any project. We must be disciplined by setting time aside to accomplish our goals. Intercessory prayer requires us to talk and be in fellowship with God regularly and consistently, so we must be a student of his word. This will help us to stay focused on the things of God so we can discern and hear the cry of someone who, while looking fine on the outside, may be going through a mental difficulty. Some people are verbally or even physically abusive in their relationships, and when they go out, they dress up and put on their best clothes, so we do not know what they are facing. But if we are consistent in prayers and fellowship with the Holy Spirit, God will show us that they have a need and place them in our hearts, so we can pray them through. When God reveals someone's situation to us, it's not for us to look at people differently or to talk about them, but it's for us to have compassion and help them.

Fourth, the Holy Ghost is the primary factor in intercessory prayer because the devil cannot interpret your thoughts, nor is he able to discern your heart. When you are interceding, your prayer language is important, so if you are not filled with the Holy Ghost, ask God to fill you so you can travail in the Spirit and birth people's deliverance. "Likewise the Spirit also helpeth our infirmities: for we know not what we should pray for as we ought: but the Spirit itself maketh intercession for us with groanings which cannot be uttered" (Romans 8:26 KJV). When you pray in the Holy Ghost, you allow your inner man to do the talking and the Holy Spirit to do the interpreting by bringing your request to God on your behalf or the behalf of others. In intercessory prayer, the Holy Ghost will take you into the enemy territory, so you can demand your enemy to drop his weapon of confusion in the lives of your family members so that they can understand the plan of God for their lives. We command the enemy to take his filthy hands off our belongings and let the people of God, who are caught up in his tactics, go free.

Last is love. Everyone wants to be loved, but not everyone is willing to go the extra miles to give love. As 1 John 4:20 (KJV) says, "If a man says, I love God, and hateth his brother, he is a liar: for he that loveth not his brother whom he hath seen, how can he love God whom he hath not seen?" Love is a part of the remedy for intercessory prayer because it was love that led Jesus to intercede and take our place on the cross, and if we are going to stand in the gap and pray for people, especially our enemies, for God to be merciful to them, love has to be embedded in our hearts. The love for a loved one should let us stay on our knees because hell is real, and too many people do not believe this concept. As believers, it is our duty to bombard heaven with prayers and cry out so that our loved one who is not in Christ can come to a true knowledge of who he is and live in him. The Bible says, "It is in him we live move and have our being" (Acts 17:28 KJV).

When we take the initiative, stand before God, and plead for someone else and ask God to hold back his wrath, I believe that touches his heart. "Most important of all, continue to show deep love for each other, for love covers a multitude of sins" (1 Peter 4:8 NLT). When you love someone, your desire is for him or her to make the right decisions. Let us be mindful of the danger of not praying. Prayer is covering, and no one in his or her right mind will go outside without first putting on the proper clothes. You would not go out in a winter jacket if it was ninety degrees outside. Likewise, no one would go outside in shorts and a T-shirt if it was below zero in the wintertime. So, we should practice not leaving our homes without first getting dressed in prayer. This means that we are to pray and cover ourselves and our loved ones every day. The Bible teaches us if we do not have love, we are nothing. Think about how great of a person you are, but if you are not filled with love in your heart, you are considered nothing in God's eyes.

The prophets spoke of God's love, but Jesus demonstrated God's love on the cross. He is our true intercessor. His ministry of intercession did not cease when he died on the cross; in fact, he's at the right hand of the Father interceding for us. Never be afraid of intervening for others because when you are praying for someone else, you are following the instructions Jesus left on record. Take note that prayer was the mantle Jesus wore on the earth and that preaching was his ministry while dying was his assignment. He fulfills his ministry, and he has accomplished his assignment, yet he still wears the prayer mantle at the right hand of the Father.

Sophia L. Garcia

Personal Testimony

I remember when I was young in the faith and did not understand the concept of gifts or calling and I was in church, and one preacher preached about the glory of God and smoke literally filling the temple. After service, I was standing in the lobby and the preacher passed by, and then he turned back and said, "Do you know how anointed you are?" I said okay, thinking, *Where is he going with this?*

He said, "When you wave your hands, people are going to feel the presence of God," so I smiled. He said, "But stop trying to figure God out!"

I said to him, "But I want to know what I am called to do. I want to know my gifts."

He said, "Don't worry about that. Just continue to do what you are doing (praying and reading the word of God) and God will use you in any area he sees fit."

I must say, I used to fast regularly and be in almost every Tuesday night prayer and Bible studies and almost every noonday prayer on Saturday. I was curious, and I had a hunger and a thirst for righteousness. I was zealous, and I wanted to know what gifts I possessed because God had used me in different areas in the ministry and I was confused. One day I would think God called me to pray and other times I would say, "Oh my, he called me to preach." Back then I did not understand how God operates through people. That was the confusing part to me because I wanted to know what gifts he had given me so I would be able to stir them up. Now I have so much joy because I said yes to God for prayer. I believe this is just the beginning of a new chapter of my life, and I understand I cannot limit God to the gift he has graced me with because he has the infinite wisdom of how to use each of us in the ministry. I believe if believers seek God and surrender their will to him, we will not be jealous of each other and wonder why we are not being used by God. I encourage each of you to surrender your way to him and let him lead and guide you and you will walk right into your destiny, bringing glory to his name in your daily walk with him.

Prayer

Heavenly Father, I pray that you will help us not to box you into the gifts that you have bless us with. Help us to know if we yield ourselves to you, you can operate through us whenever there is a need in someone's life. Forgive us for putting limitations on you. Help us not to be frustrated because of the holding place you have us in. Lord, we need you. Please help us to understand you are bigger than the assignment, the call, and the plans you have for our lives in Jesus's name. Amen.

Intercession of a Friend

Mark gives us a perfect illustration of what true friendship is made of, especially in a time of need. Chapter 2:2-11 (NIV) says,

> A few days later, when Jesus again entered Capernaum, the people heard that he had come home. They gathered in such large numbers that there was no room left, not even outside the door, and he preached the word to them. Four men came carrying a paralyzed man. Since they could not get him to Jesus because of the crowd, they made an opening in the roof above Jesus by digging through

it and then lowered the mat the man was lying on. When Jesus saw their faith, he said to the paralyzed man, "Son, your sins are forgiven." Now, some teachers of the law were sitting there thinking to themselves, "Why does this fellow talk like that? He's blaspheming! Who can forgive sins but God alone?" Immediately, Jesus knew in his spirit that this was what they were thinking in their hearts, and he said to them, "Why are you thinking these things? Which is easier: to say to this paralyzed man, 'Your sins are forgiven' or to say, 'Get up, take your mat and walk'? I want you to know that the Son of Man has the authority on earth to forgive sins. So, he said to the man, 'I tell you, get up, take your mat, and go home.' He got up, took his mat, and walked out in full view of them all. This amazed everyone, and they praised God, saying, 'We have never seen anything like this!'"

After examining the scripture, we can conclude that those four men knew the only person who could heal their friend was Jesus. They probably felt that this was a once-in-a-lifetime opportunity. Jesus was back in Capernaum, and this time his friends were going to make their efforts worth something because when Jesus was in town, everybody came to hear him whether they agreed with his teaching or not. His friends did not get the opportunity to be in the house upon Jesus's arrival. Perhaps they had to convince the paralyzed man to go to Jesus, and he was so caught up in his circumstances, which clouded his mind, that he did not think it was possible to be heal. Or maybe they had prayed before and nothing had happened because he was in disbelief. For someone's deliverance to take place, faith must be in operation.

> For someone's deliverance to take place, faith must be in operation.

Therefore, we should be careful about whom we connect to and choose our friends wisely, because when it's time to believe God, you don't need someone to question you and ask, "Did you hear from God?"

Thus, this time, the paralyzed man's friends were not going to allow him to stay in doubt, and the fact that he was not able to walk did not seem bothersome. They tolerated all his controversy because they knew Jesus could change the outcome of his situation. For this reason, they joined their faiths together with one purpose in mind: their friend needed healing, and it was going to happen that day. When they got to the house where Jesus was, they did not let the size of the crowd deter them from getting to him, nor did they let obstacles stop them from climbing the roof.

Sometimes, we make what we are going through downplay our efforts, and we forget that the journey we are on is getting to Jesus. For this reason, we should not let anything stop us from reaching our goal. With determination and a love for their friend, they made a grand entrance into the presence of Jesus.

Indeed, this was not an easy task carrying a grown man to Jesus on a hot day. Also, they had to climb to the top of the roof, cut out space, and make room for him to fit through so he could receive his deliverance. It's not always easy to labor with someone, especially when it's time for us to carry each other's burdens to the master in prayer. Take note it was the friends' faith that got Jesus's attention. Jesus pointed out the importance of their faith. He wanted believers to understand that it is a part of a Christian's duty to carry his or her brother or sister to the Father in prayer. (Read Galatians 6:2)

When we see someone, whose faith has been tested to the point that his or her belief in God has been crippled, we must intercede for him or her until his or her strength and faith have been renewed. Although the paralyzed man's condition was physical, some people are in the same predicament today spiritually.

They are bound by sins, or they let Satan play guilt trips on their minds. It's our responsibility as intercessors to bring them to Jesus and war in prayer until their deliverance takes place. We may be ready to give up on people because their faith is not as strong as ours, and we say, "Well, it depends on them. I did all I could by telling them what Jesus can do for them in their situation. It's up to them to believe in God for themselves." However, I beg to differ because clearly, we see in the scriptures that this is not always the case. For some people, deliverance depends on others' faith.

Personal Testimony

A couple of years ago, I got the urge from the Holy Ghost to pray for a close person who was dear to my heart. I called her, but she did not pick up the phone. So that Saturday afternoon, I went to her house to find out how she was doing. I let her know I felt led to come over to pray for her, not knowing that she had a heart condition and was going to have open-heart surgery on Monday.

At that time, I did not understand what it means to pray, but because I trusted God, I asked her, "Will you allow me to pray with you for a few minutes?" I opened my mouth and began to pray, and to my surprise, the Holy Ghost took over, and I began to intercede on her behalf. I knew it was God because I had never prayed like that before, nor had I experienced the power of God like that in prayer before.

On Monday morning, my friend went in for surgery. The doctors did their last check just to make sure she was healthy for the operation. While they were prepping her, they realized she did not need to have open-heart surgery anymore because God had performed a miracle. I give God all the glory for using me to bless her life. You don't have to be afraid if you are sick in your body because God still heals. As Bishop Gil would say, God will let you live with what other people died from if you trust him.

Prayer

Father, I pray for people who are sick in their bodies and don't know what to do. Lord, touch their bodies right now and cause them to respond to prayer because you are the great physician. God, there is nothing too hard for you. Give them the strength to meditate on your word so their faith will be strong. In Jesus's name, amen!

An Urgent Request

In the United States of America, people's lives are in a state of uncertainty because of the government trying to repeal or replace the Affordable Care Act, otherwise known as Obamacare, which so many people in the country depend on. If such a law is passed, I believe the country will experience great turmoil when people lose their insurance benefits, especially those with preexisting conditions. Can you imagine if people are sick and not able to get the care they need or cannot afford to pay for their medication? The government doesn't know what to do, and the people don't know what to expect. I think the Democrats and the Republicans should put their differences aside for the American people. Because Obamacare is already in effect, some think it's working while others think it's a disaster.

Personally, with my experience working in the medical field, I understand that not having insurance can be detrimental. I really believe Obamacare is fixable, and both parties should come together for a common cause. This is why it is crucial for us, the people of God, to try our best to stay in tune with the Father, because we never know when someone is going to have an urgent request. At that moment, we need to take on their burdens, tap into the spiritual realm, and allow prayer to God to mend their brokenness. Being prepared spiritually is a must, and we cannot afford not to be prepared. EMS employees do not know for sure if there is going to be an emergency. They just show up for work in case a call comes in so they can dispatch police officers, an ambulance, or fire trucks to where they are needed.

Have you ever been driving and heard an ambulance but had no clue which direction it was coming from? Your first instinct is to get out of the way because you were taught that when you hear an emergency vehicle, you should move over so the path will be free. You may not understand the severity of the incident, but you know there has been some type of emergency, whether a person is inside the ambulance or is waiting for the ambulance to arrive.

Jesus was not driving an ambulance, nor was he an EMS employee, but he was on the scene where there was an emergency. A Roman soldier had a dying need, and his master had an urgent request. The scripture reveals

When Jesus entered Capernaum, He was approach by Jewish leaders explaining that he needed to visit the house of a centurion's servant, whom his master valued highly, was sick and about to die. The centurion had heard of the miracles of Jesus, so when his servant was sick, he had no problem sending some elders of the Jews to Jesus to ask Him to come and heal his servant. When they came to Jesus, they pleaded earnestly with Him. "This man deserves to have you do this because he loves our nation and has built our synagogue." So Jesus went with them. Jesus was not far from the house when the centurion sent friends to say to Him, "Lord, don't trouble yourself, for I do not deserve to have you come under my roof. That is why I did not even consider myself worthy to come to you. But say the word, and my servant will be healed. For I am a man under authority, with soldiers under me. I tell this one, 'Go,' and he goes; and that one, 'Come,' and he comes. I say to my servant, 'Do this,' and he does it." When Jesus heard this, he was amazed at him and turning to the crowd following him, He said, "I tell you, I have not found such great faith even in Israel." Then the men who had been sent returned to the house and found the servant well. (Luke 7:2–10 NIV)

Notice that when the elders approached Jesus, they started explaining what the centurion had done for the Jewish people. They brought this to his attention because they knew Solomon had built a temple and commissioned the people to worship God. They understood the concept of worship, that it invites God in and gives him opportunities to perform miracles. Building a place of worship is a prerequisite for healing. James told us that if any among us are sick, we can call on the elders of the church. Read James 5:14.

Bishop Anthony W. Gilyard is teaching the congregation to be silent no more. One of the first things he taught us was to establish a place in our homes where we can meet with God every day, preferably at the same time each day. Once we go into covenant with God, he keeps his word, so we have a guarantee that God will be showing up at that established place.

There is no doubt that his teaching on silent no more is significant. It means that our pastor sees the need for the church to return to its rightful place as a house of prayer. One way to get a breakthrough in prayer is to respect authority. We have to respect those we sit under because we don't know when a situation will arise in our lives when we will need them to send a request to Jesus—not any request but an urgent one on our behalf.

In the story of the centurion, the slave was not just obedient to his master. He probably went above and beyond his call of duty. His master forgot about himself and the position he sat in. After all, he could have just replaced that slave. But perhaps he was not just any slave to his master; his master cared about him. Notice that the centurion sent the elders because he had faith in their God. You should not be so preoccupied with your position that it hinders you from reaching out for help. Acknowledging the need for help is a sign of humility and not weakness.

> *You should not be so preoccupied with your position that it hinders you from reaching out for help. Acknowledging the need for help is a sign of humility and not weakness.*

The centurion made it known that he understood the chain of command when Jesus recommended house visitation. He told Jesus that he was a man under authority, so Jesus did not need to visit his place of residence. He could just send the word, demonstrating the power of the spoken word. The centurion stood in the gap for the one who was serving him, which shows compassion because our position should not make us lord over people; it should make us concerned about the well-being of individuals. However, one thing is certainly clear: Jesus moves on faith. We must not go to Jesus and ask him to do anything without first believing that he can do the impossible. The centurion had wealth and power, but neither his money nor his position could heal his servant. The centurion soldier understood that military strength was not going to win the battle against sickness, so he had to send for the one who has the authority over all things, including disease. Often, we think our position gives us access to a miracle. Take note that the miracle could not be manifested without faith.

> *We must not go to Jesus and ask him to do anything without first believing that he can do the impossible*

Personal Testimony

About seven years ago, I found myself in a financial dilemma. In other words, I had an urgent request. It felt as if someone had put weights on my shoulders. I was full of anxiety, and I had trouble sleeping. One night while I was asleep, the scripture kept ringing in my ears: "Take no thought for tomorrow" (Matthew 6:34 NIV). I literally jumped out of my sleep and thought to myself I didn't know I was so worried about what I was going through.

I had a rental property, and the tenants were not paying their rent. My payments on the mortgage on the house I was living in had fallen behind because I was paying the mortgage on the rental property. During this time, my husband had lost his job, and we were not able to pay our bills on time. During all this, people were calling me to pray for them because they were going to be put out of their apartments or their houses were going into foreclosure. I would say to myself, *If they only knew I was in the same situation.* After praying, I would stretch out on the floor and cry out to God, asking him, "Who is praying for me?" But I had to intercede on my own behalf. I knew the pastor was also praying because I had told him about my situation. In the home modifications process, I was told by my lawyer to file for bankruptcy and give up the house where I resided. So, we did. Because of the bankruptcy, the bank repossessed my car, which I had one year left to pay on. This was a trying time in my life. I felt like a failure, but I kept on believing in God. Within a couple of months, the court dismissed the bankruptcy, and I was asked if I wanted my car back. I said no because the car dealer had already sold it and there was too much paperwork involved. After five years, the bank that had the mortgage wanted to give us our house back. I realized that sometimes you must let go of some things so you can gain more or get something bigger or better. Although the court had dismissed the bankruptcy, my credit was ruined, and I was not able to purchase anything without the interest rate being around 14 percent. I had to keep a smile on my face because I knew people were watching my life, and I believe if I had started acting as if God did not exist, my previous testimony on how God had delivered me before would have been in vain.

During my time of affliction, a voice spoke to me and said, "I'm in control, and I do whatever I want to do whenever I want to." I accepted his words and built up enough courage to look into the mirror and say, "Devil, God knew I was going to be in the situation before I was even born, so I'm not sweating it. Girl, this light affliction is but for a moment." I continued to say those words to myself until I started believing. I was still going to church every Sunday, hoping that someone would call me out and minister to me. But God had other plans and he wanted me to trust him.

I felt life was unfair because my husband's employer had wrongfully fired him, and he was not being paid unemployment for the time he was out because they were investigating. I told my husband not to look for a job because they had to give him his old job back because firing him without a valid reason gave God a platform for a miracle for his child. My husband is a man who loves to provide for his family, so he was looking for work. I kept on telling him he should use that time to get closer to the Lord. About two months later, my husband found a job, and at the end of his first week with his new employer, his old employer called him back.

One morning I decide to meet God at five-thirty for prayer. While I was kneeling, I felt the Holy Ghost was leading me to bind up financial demons. I was a little hesitant at first to say it out loud, but now it has become a part of my prayer because sometimes we don't have the faith to believe. But if we continue to seek God, our faith will grow.

Prayer

Father, I thank you for what you have allowed me to experience. Thank you for not letting me give up on you or myself. I pray that you will touch the heart that's reading this right now and minister in the area where this person needs it most. Thank you for listening and answering. In Jesus's name, amen.

Sophia L. Garcia

Giving Ownership Back to God

> One of the greatest things we can do while praying is to give ownership back to God,

One of the greatest things we can do while praying is to give ownership back to God, because when you are interceding, the enemy sees you as a threat, and he will use anything or anyone to disrupt your flow. The enemy will use the spirit of fear and discouragement to keep you from praying. But we cannot allow the enemy to boycott our mission. As intercessors, our task is to pray and fight in the spirit realm until God destroys the enemy's plot. We cannot give up, and we cannot quit. Our assignment is to be the watch of men and women on the wall. We need to tune in to God so much that even when we sleep, our spirit can watch.

Moses, the great intercessor, did not waste the moment when he was faced with a hard decision after God took his people out of Egypt. God called Moses to have a one-on-one meeting so he could give him instructions on how the people should live their lives and be a holy nation. While Moses was getting the commandments from God, the people became impatient, and instead of waiting for Moses to come back from his glorious experience with the Lord, they asked Aaron to make them an idol in the form of a god.

> When Moses didn't come back down the mountain right away, the people went to Aaron. "Look," they said, "make us a god to lead us, for this fellow Moses who brought us here from Egypt has disappeared; something must have happened to him." "Give me your gold earrings," Aaron replied. So they all did—men and women, boys and girls. Aaron melted the gold, then molded and tooled it into the form of a

calf. The people exclaimed, "O Israel, this is the god that brought you out of Egypt. Then the Lord told Moses, "Quick! Go on down, for your people that you brought from Egypt have defiled themselves, and have quickly abandoned all my laws. They have molded themselves a calf, and worshiped it, and sacrificed to it, and said, 'This is your god, O Israel, that brought you out of Egypt.'" Then the Lord said, "I have seen what a stubborn, rebellious lot these people are. Now leave me alone and my anger shall blaze out against them and destroy them all; and I will make you, Moses, into a great nation instead of them." But Moses begged God not to do it. "Lord," he pleaded, "why is your anger so hot against your own people whom you brought from the land of Egypt with such great power and mighty miracles? Do you want the Egyptians to say, 'God tricked them into coming to the mountains so that he could slay them, destroying them from off the face of the earth'? Turn back from your fierce wrath. Turn away from this terrible evil you are planning against your people! Remember your promise to your servants—to Abraham, Isaac, and Israel. For you swore by your own self, 'I will multiply your posterity as the stars of heaven, and I will give them all of this land I have promised to your descendants, and they shall inherit it forever.'" So the Lord changed his mind and spared them. (Exodus 32:1–2, 7–14 TLB)

What a great example of an intercessor. Moses pleaded with

God because God told him he was going to destroy the people and raise Moses up, but as an intercessor, you do not think about yourself only. You regularly reflect on how to cry out to God that someone else might be free. Moses put the ownership back on God and reminded him that the people were his responsibility. If God destroyed the people, the Egyptians would think that God could not do what he had promised. Sometimes when we go to God in prayer, we must have the goal to put ownership back on God and remind him of his word. God takes pride in his word. Moses knew God could not go back on his word. Moses was standing in the gap, shielding the people, and God changed his mind. This is a typical example of an intercessor, an individual who is willing to sacrifice his or her time and have a conversation with God about another person's well-being. There are times when we might not know what words to say or what to do in prayer, but we can always remind God of his word. As an intercessor, you must be a carrier of the word of God in your spirit. If you do not memorize and study as well as meditate on God's word, you cannot remind God of his word. When the devil tempted Jesus in the wilderness, Jesus did not fall to his plot. He fought the enemy by using the word of God. (Read Matthew 4.)

The word of God is vital in prayer, especially in intercessory prayer. When warring in prayer, we must also remind the devil of what the word of God says. Whatever you are believing God about—for example, if it's healing, find the scripture that pertains to your needs and pray his words back to him. If God has promised you something and it has not come to pass yet, make sure you are not the hindrance to your own promises.

> The word of God is vital in prayer, especially in intercessory prayer.

Personal Testimony

I remember when the spirit of God was leading me to leave my former church. My husband and I were not in agreement. In fact, he told me that he was not leaving, so we were going to two different churches, and we took turns bringing our son to church with us. This was overwhelming to me, so I went to God in prayer, and I put the ownership back on him. I said, "God, you do not split up families, so I am asking you to fix this." I am not saying that husband and wife cannot worship at two different churches, but for me it was personal; this was between God and me. Not only did my husband come to first day the church opened, but he is also an ordained deacon at the church I am a member of. A couple of years later, he told me that when he used to drive the church van and pick up the mothers for Sunday school at our former church, they would say, "Many people leave the church for the wrong reason, but not your wife." I was in awe of God because that let me know God had my back.

Prayer

Father, I pray in the name of Jesus that you will help me to understand your word and to know that I can apply it to my situation. Father, let your word come alive in my heart. In Jesus's name, amen.

5

What's the Cost of Your Worship?

> But the hour is coming, and now is, when the true worshipers will worship the Father in spirit and truth; for the Father is seeking such to worship Him. God is Spirit, and those who worship Him must worship in spirit and truth. (John 4:23–24 KJV)

We have heard the saying that nothing in life is free. If you want something, you are going to have to give something. Someone may say, "I beg to differ because salvation is free." But my question to you is, is salvation really free when Jesus, the Son of God, was betrayed by one of his disciples for thirty pieces of silver? This is why we have to be careful about whom we worship with. So many people are in church, but they are not giving God true worship. If our friends are true worshipers, they will not turn their backs on us in times of crisis.

Worship is priceless because none of us can compensate Jesus for what he did on the cross. But we can express our love for him through worship by thanking him for what he has done and giving him true worship. True worship divulges sinfulness, accept the grace that God has freely offered us, acknowledges his holiness, and surrender our lives so he can use us.

> *True worship divulges sinfulness, accept the grace that God has freely offered us, acknowledges his holiness, and surrender our lives so he can use us.*

Worship comes from the Anglo-Saxon *weorthscipe,* which meant to ascribe worth, to pay homage, to reverence or venerate. It was modified to worthship and then to worship. It refers to worth or worthiness. (Growing Towards Spiritual Maturity Page 47) So then, we can conclude that worship is not the way we sing or the way we pray or even the way we dress. If we are praying using vain repetition, it's like giving God lip service and wearing garments out of ritual. These things will not bring glory or honor to God. Worship is a lifestyle. Worship is what you do when nobody's watching your everyday routine. It is the expression of yourself to the Almighty God through reverence. It is a daily sacrifice of your mind, body, and soul to God. Worship separates you from the ordinary and gives you a one-on-one with God. Matthew paints a portrait for us to see that we can worship God with what's valuable even though someone else may see it as useless:

> When Jesus was at the party of Simon's house there came unto him a woman having an alabaster box of very precious ointment, and poured it on his head, as he sat at meat. But when his disciples saw

it, they had indignation, saying, To what purpose is this waste? For this ointment might have been sold for much, and given to the poor. When Jesus understood it, he said unto them, Why trouble ye the woman? For she hath wrought a good work upon me. For ye have the poor always with you, but me ye have not always. For in that she hath poured this ointment on my body, she did it for my burial. Verily, I say unto you, wheresoever this gospel shall be preached in the whole world, there shall also this, that this woman hath done, be told for a memorial of her. (Matthew 26:6–13 KJV)

This woman can be put into these three categories: silly, strange, and pure.

Silly Worship

It's funny how people can see you doing something, and because they don't understand or cannot relate, they draw their own conclusions. The disciples thought that because the ointment was so precious, the woman was silly to be wasting it. Although her worship seemed silly, she did not mind looking that way because she was not a spectator; she was a worshiper who was bold enough to approach Jesus because he was approachable.

Everyone is not going to understand the way you worship, and that's okay because everyone should have their own style of worship. The disciples who walked with Jesus did not understand what he was worth at that moment. Sometimes we have valuable treasures in our lives, and because of their value, we miss our moment, but nothing is more valuable than having Jesus in our presence. The important thing is that you recognize when he is in your midst because some worship centers quench the Spirit and allow man to be praised. The disciples understood the value of the alabaster box, but they did not understand the concept and the importance of its use and were unable to discern the meaning of the woman's worship. I believe the disciples found her to be a silly woman, weak in intellect because she should have been able to see that this was a prestigious occasion and that outcasts were not invited. Ironically, she was at the right place at the right time because Simon was a leper, and lepers were considered rejects. Perhaps they thought she was mentally challenged because if she were in her right mind, she would not have possibly wasted the jar of oil that was worth a year's savings on Jesus. What the disciples did not understand was that to this woman, Jesus was worth all her worship and praise. She was ready to accept the one true God, who was manifested in the flesh (John 1:14).

Notice that her worship disturbed the disciples. They were angry and upset about someone giving Jesus worship. It is the same in churches today when you are worshiping beyond the norm of clapping hands or nodding heads. For example, if someone is worshiping by crying out or running around the church, some people may want the service to move on to what's next on the program because they may think the person is acting out of the ordinary way church service should be conducted. The worship of God may sometimes seem silly, and you must press beyond people's opinion of you to get through to God at times. When you worship God, you get Jesus's attention, so when you are praying, especially during church services, you must stay focused and block out everything that may distract you, making God your focus. Only you know what you are going through and what you need God to do for you. No one can satisfy the hunger in your soul, and no one can cleanse you as thoroughly as God can.

To worship, you must first offer a sacrifice. The Old Testament makes it clear that God required animal sacrifices. These animals had to be slain on the altar and offered to God, but after they died, they were no longer useful to him. We don't have to bring a lamb to the altar anymore, and we don't have to perform an atonement once a year, but God still requires sacrifice. Romans 12:1(KJV) states, "I beseech you, therefore, brethren, by the mercies of God, that ye present your bodies a living sacrifice, holy, acceptable unto God, which is your reasonable service." The law of the Old Testament that required the children of Israel to perform animal sacrifices every year to atone for their sins was temporal until Jesus became that Lamb once and for all by making the ultimate sacrifice. No longer are the children of God required to bring animal sacrifices to be slain on the altar, which represents a dead sacrifice. Thus, we are living in the dispensation of grace, and God wants us to present our bodies daily as the living sacrifice. This is a sacrifice that's acceptable and pleasing to him.

When you offer yourself up to him, he can touch you in your most vulnerable place: your soul. He's not looking for a sacrifice that is offered up to be burned on the altar with no fellowship; he wants fellowship that can be obtained through prayer and worship. We can all learn from the woman who decided to worship regardless. Thus, I say to you today that whatever barrier you need to cross to worship, make up your mind and cross that barrier fearlessly. Keep in mind that the only person's attention you need is Jesus's, and as long as he's pleased, you have done your due diligence.

Personal Testimony

I must admit that my worship at BJCF sometimes seems silly. I used to wonder what people thought of me, but I have grown to be comfortable in my worship because I understand the importance of the atmosphere. Sometimes people come in with different types of spirits, so I'm called to intercede. I have learned that I am not just interceding on behalf of people but also for the atmosphere in our services. If God calls you to do a task out of the ordinary, don't be afraid. Just worship and let him have his way.

Prayer

Father, in the name of Jesus, I come to you today because I need you. I pray that you will help me to be more vulnerable in your presence and to let go of dead sacrifices. Oh God, the things I do that have no value to you. Help me, Lord, to present my body as a living sacrifice so I can go where you commission me to go. Father, I lay aside the sins and weight that cause me to sin against you in Jesus's name. Empty me of myself, so I can be filled with your presence.

Strange Worship

When you are in a church setting, people believe that worship is restricted to a certain way. Of course, this statement can be true. It depends on what denomination you worship in. For instance, this lady was under the Jewish law, so perhaps someone else might have though that, this is a strange woman because common sense should have told her that when she is in the presence of a man, she should not flaunt herself in front of him, especially in public. However, sometimes, to get through to worship, you are going to have to do some strange things that people might not understand. But that's between you and your God.

One Sunday, God might tell you during church service, "I want you to lay on the altar." This is where maturity comes in—you cannot worry about what people will think of you. For example, a woman went to the altar when the pastor was preaching because she felt she had to be there. This woman also interrupted a dinner party at Simon's house by pouring out her love for Jesus. She ruined the party for some by making it about Jesus and her. This woman action shows worship is a personal thing and we do not need someone choreographing our worship.

Her heart moved her to prepare Jesus's body for burial. Her name was not on the guest list, nor did she belong to the elite, but she had a purpose to fulfill. She knew that this man was going to die on the cross for her sins, and she just wanted to show her appreciation. The scriptures give no indication that words were coming out of her mouth, but judging by her actions, one can assume that she was saying, "I don't know how much it will cost, and I know I can never repay you, but I've been waiting for this moment to be in your presence." She wasted a year's worth of savings just for one moment in the presence of the savior.

> We cannot worship God and ourselves at the same time. He takes pleasure in our glorification of him.

What will you give to have an audience with the Savior? If we are going to have an audience with God, first we must forget about ourselves because we cannot worship God and ourselves at the same time. He takes pleasure in our glorification of him. We must also understand that this woman had to cross barriers for an audience with Jesus. First, she was a woman, and second, she was a sinner. She was an outsider, but she found her way to a unique place because of her worship. There is uninterrupted worship going on in heaven, but when believers start worshiping, we literally join in to the heavenly worship by getting God's attention. We do not stop the angels from worshiping, but God turns his attention to his children when he hears worship. (Read John 9:31)

> What is man, that thou art mindful of him? And the son of man, that thou visitest him? For thou hast made him a little lower than the angels, and hast crowned him with glory and honor. (Psalm 8:4–6 KJV)

Worship allows God to see inside you. The hour is coming, and it is then that true worshipers will worship the Father in spirit and truth, for the Father is seeking such people to worship him. Are you one of the people God is seeking to worship him? Will you accept the call to worship? For those who worship him must do so in spirit and truth. It may look strange to others, but God knows what you must offer, so forget about the fault-finders and give God your most precious gem, which is your true worship.

Personal Testimony

I had an experience once when the Spirit of God told me to lay my hand on a mother in the church, and I was reluctant to do it. It took me a couple of minutes before I went over to her because I was sitting at the pulpit and the pastor was talking to the congregation. I felt it was a little strange because the congregation was staring at me, and I was not following protocol. Eventually, I gathered courage and laid my hands on her, and both of us started praising God. Something great happened after we finished. The pastor told the mother she was healed and to hug another mother, who would get her healing too. It was a relief because the saints were looking at me strangely, but I felt that God honored my obedience to him. It's still a challenge to obey the voice of God, but I am comfortable in his presence, and I yield to whatever strange way he wants me to worship.

Prayer

Father, I pray I will not miss out on the opportunity to be in your presence. Help me to seize the moment and worship you every day because you deserve all my worship, and you are worthy of all my praise all day long. Remove anything I put in your place; strip me from all unrighteousness. Oh God, my worship may be strange to others, but accept my true worship in Jesus's name.

Pure Worship

The woman with the oil went against the odds to give Jesus pure worship. It may have cost her reputation, but she kept on worshiping. It caused her to be criticized, but she kept on worshiping. It caused her to be hated, but she kept on worshiping. The people around her did not understand that in worship, you can be liberated. We all need to realize that what we go through should not affect our worship. I know it's not easy to worship when things are not going the way we want them to go. However, as believers, we need to know that worship draws the spirit of God closer to us so we may worship him every chance we get. The woman with the oil had one purpose: to worship the Messiah, the one true God in the flesh. Jesus was pleased with her worship because she blocked out everyone and everything just to worship him. Perhaps she was so caught up in her worship that she forgot about who she was and where she was. This type of worship got Jesus's attention, and he proclaimed that wherever the gospel was preached would be a memorial to her.

What would Jesus say about your worship? Is your worship going up as a sweet-smelling fragrance, or is it a stench in his nostrils? Is your worship costing you anything? If it isn't, you must examine your heart and make sure it's prepared and ready to worship God. The enemy is going to try everything in his power to keep you from worshiping. One of his best tools is distraction because we are his replacement. Lucifer was one of the angels who also worshiped before the throne, but he wanted to be like God, so his pride cost him his position in heaven. No longer was he required to bow and declare, "Holy, Holy, Holy," to the Lord God Almighty. Isaiah said of Lucifer, "You said in your heart, 'I will ascend to the heavens; I will raise my throne above the stars of God; I will sit enthroned on the mount of assembly, on the utmost heights of Mount Zaphon'" (Isaiah 14:13 NIV).

The book of Revelation goes on to say,

> And war broke out in heaven: Michael and his angels fought against the dragon; and the dragon and his angels fought, but they did not prevail, nor was a place found for them in heaven any longer. So the great dragon was cast out, that serpent of old, called the Devil and Satan, who deceives the whole world; he was cast to the earth, and his angels were cast out with him. (Revelation 12:8–9 KJV)

Lucifer got in trouble with God because he thought too much of himself. When you elevate yourself over the Creator, it will break and then destroy the relationship you have with God. Worship and prayer are important because they will keep your spirit humble before God. It is a constant reminder that God is involved in every area of our lives. Not all of us are going to be called to be worship leaders or stand in front of the congregation to usher people into the presence of God, but we can all worship at home, at school, or even at work by making melodies in our hearts without making a public display. Worship is your willingness to surrender all the issues of your heart to God. There is a position available in heaven with no experience required because the Holy Ghost is willing to do on-the-job training. If you want to have an audience with God, keep your heart clear of offense and stay in continuous worship. Take the initiative to be the person who is willing to reconcile and be the peacemaker so your worship will not be contaminated.

Personal Testimony

I used to be afraid of the presence of God, but I eventually grew to be comfortable with it. I had an experience when I was in church one Sunday morning when my spirit left my body. When I came back, I was so disappointed. I realized I was still in the church. I began to praise God. This experience made me want to go to heaven even more because the place my spirit visited was very peaceful.

Prayer

Father, in the name of Jesus, I ask that you allow the person reading this now to experience your presence. Your presence can be felt anywhere, so God, give this person a yearning in his or her soul for you. Help me keep my heart in tune with you so I can worship you, Lord. Father, forgive me for all the offenses I have caused to others and the offenses that others have caused to me. I pray that nothing hinders my worship today. Amen!

6

Silent No More

> I have posted watchmen on your walls, Jerusalem; they will never be silent day or night. You who call on the LORD, give yourselves no rest. (Isaiah 62:6 NIV)

If we are going to be silent no more, we must be in position and stay in the throne room. In the throne room, you should be skillful in prayer by allowing the Holy Ghost to be in total control. In the throne room, your native language cannot be the language of the day. You need the Holy Ghost so you can tap into the heavenly languages and speak in an unknown tongue. When you are praying in unknown tongues, the devil does not know what you are praying for, so he will not understand the blessings God releases, and he will not have victory over you because you are charged and ready for spiritual warfare. Can you imagine if the body of Christ took God up on his challenge and decided to be silent no more by wearing God out in prayer? I know we cannot get on God's nerves, but the thought of our praying every minute of every hour seems like something we would enjoy and God would approve of. We could at least try by having a prayer chain where at least forty-eight people, where we have two dedicated people every hour who will stand watch and pray around the clock. Now, that would be amazing. I believe we will bring heaven on earth through the manifestation of God's presence having a domino effect across the globe. This does not have to be merely thought about; it can be a reality. The Bible declares let "His will be done on earth as it is in heaven" (Matthew 6:10 KJV).

But if we are going to be silent no more, someone must be willing to sound the alarm and become a risk-taker. Thus, it cannot be just one person; it has to be a group effort. For example, churches of different denominations not only all believe, but all have a relationship with God the Father; Jesus, the Son of God; and the working power of the Holy Ghost. I did not grow up in church, but I heard people testify to the presence of the power of God in the church of yesteryear. To my understanding, we are still serving the same God, and Hebrews 13:8 (KJV) says he changes not. My question to the believers is, what happens to those who do not follow God's will on the earth or maybe are in the category of spiritual dropouts? The good thing about being a spiritual dropout is that we can run back into the presence of our Father and be welcome. Luke 15:11-32 shows how the parable of the prodigal son demonstrated the forgiveness of a loving father. Although his son left home, wasted all his substances and forgot about his family for a season; his father welcomed him back with open arms. Thus, we can identify true forgiveness of God's restoration to all who have walked away from God. God is waiting with open arms to restore back to himself. God will not only restore you back into fellowship but he will restore you back to your original place in him. The prodigal son's father did not make him one of his hired servant he reinstated him as a son.

> "Come now, let us settle the matter," says the LORD. "Though your sins are like scarlet, they shall be as white as snow; though they are red as crimson, they shall be as wool." (Isaiah 1:19 NIV)

God is always looking to have a relationship with his creation, and being silent no more means building up our relationship with God. The more we pray, the better we can overcome our flesh. If we are going to at least try to overcome our flesh, we must have discipline and consistency; the more disciplined we are, the easier it is for God to mold us. If we are going to be silent no more, we cannot allow our thoughts to hijack our prayer lives. The moment we decide to pray, all sorts of ideas enter our minds, and if we are not careful, we will let our minds wander instead of praying. I have no doubt that Jesus faced the same scenario, but he did not give into his thoughts or the mind games of the enemy.

> The moment we decide to pray, all sorts of ideas enter our minds, and if we are not careful, we will let our minds wander instead of praying.

If you go off track, prayer will get you back on track. It's not as hard as you think. It's just like having an old friend you haven't spoken with in a long time, and you wonder whether you should dial his or her number. You contemplate it for days, and suddenly, you've got enough courage to call. By the time you finish talking, it seems as if the last conversation you had was just yesterday. Now picture it the same way with God, and just start talking.

First, take a moment, and just start to acknowledge him by

giving him adoration. Tell him how great he is and how wonderful he has been in your life. Pay tribute to him, read the book of Psalms to increase your vocabulary, and get to know him better with the different experiences of the kings, prophets, and ordinary people. While you are reading the Psalms, you will gain an understanding of his attributes and how you can better your relationship with him.

> Lord, our Lord, how majestic is your name in all the earth! You have set your glory in the heavens. Through the praise of children and infants, you have established a stronghold against your enemies, to silence the foe and the avenger. When I consider your heavens, the work of your fingers, the moon, and the stars, which you have set in place. (Psalm 8:1-3 NIV)

Second, we must confess our sins to keep our relationship fresh with the Lord. First John 1:9 (KJV) says, "If we confess our sins, he is faithful and just to forgive us our sins, and to cleanse us from all unrighteousness." Be specific with him, and let him know how sorry you are about going against his will because sins will cause you to renege on your relationship with God. We will not write him a resignation letter, but our attitude toward him will change, thus causing us to withdraw our service to him. The relationship with the Father is everlasting. It's a relationship guaranteed to last for eternity if you want it to. Don't give up. Let us not be repeat offenders. At some point, we need to examine ourselves and let God know we're at fault and don't want to continue down the wrong path. God is a God of mercy, and he welcomes anyone who is ready to change their ways. So, ask him to keep you from daily temptation because when we are in a right standing with God, we bring glory to his name, thus giving people an opportunity to see him in us.

Third, we are to be thankful. Psalm 107:1 (NIV) says, "Give thanks to the LORD, for he is good; his love endures forever." God's goodness supersedes anything that we encounter in our life. It is God's goodness that leads us to repentance. The mere fact that God allowed his Son, Jesus, to die on the cross to redeem us is enough to be thankful.

For God to wake us up and give us another day should cause us to be thankful. Every day, someone goes home to eternity, but God adds another day to our journey. Sometimes our journey seems longer than expected because of what we are facing, but if we take a moment, despite what we are going through, and thank him, our lives will have greater meaning. Thanking God propels us into his presence, and in his presence is the fullness of joy, and the joy of the Lord is our strength. It is a trick of the enemy for us not to be thankful. When you are pleased, it will lead you to be grateful, and gratefulness causes you to see your heavenly Father in a different light, and you get to understand that it is because of his mercy that you are still in your right state of mind. "In everything give thanks. This is what God wants you to do because of Christ Jesus" (1 Thessalonians 5:18 NIV).

Fourth, make your supplication known unto him. Also, our requests should come from the right motives. "When you ask and you do not receive, it is because you ask with the wrong motives, that you may spend what you get on your pleasures" (James 4:3 NIV). We cannot ask for things because we want people to see what we have. We must make our requests with others in mind. Whatever we ask of God should also be a blessing to someone else.

In Ephesians 6:18 (NIV), the writer encourages us to "Pray in the Spirit at all times and on every occasion. Stay alert and be persistent in your prayers for all believers everywhere." It is essential for us to pray for one another because prayer encourages us. It's encouraging to know that someone is praying for you. Whatever you do today, don't forget to make requests on someone else's behalf.

Last, although prayer is personal, it is vital that you get a prayer partner. Have someone whom you are accountable to and for you. Matthew recorded the words of Jesus in 18:19–20 (NIV): "Again, truly I tell you that if two of you on earth agree about anything they ask for, it will be done for them by my Father in heaven. For where two or three gather in my name, there am I with them." Sometimes because of what we are going through or because our faith becomes weak and we become complacent and discouraged, we are reluctant to pray. In this season of life, we need to have someone who can carry our burdens to the Lord. Proverbs 27:17 (NIV) says, "As iron sharpens iron, so one person sharpens another." When you rub two knives together, they both benefit because one supports the other. It is the same in our spiritual lives. If you have a prayer partner, you both will reap the benefits of victories through prayer. Prayer will cause you to grow and become more effective in your individual walk with God. Paul and Silas experienced the benefits of victory in Acts 16:26 (NIV) "About midnight Paul and Silas were praying and singing hymns to God, and the other prisoners were listening to them. Suddenly there was such a violent earthquake that the foundations of the prison were shaken. At once all the prison doors flew open, and everyone's chains came loose." This is a strong example of the power of a prayer partner. Having someone to partner with in prayer is a blessing because not only will your partner be blessed by your prayer, but people around you will also reap the benefits. Let us connect with a partner in prayer so we can effect

> *Sometimes because of what we are going through or because our faith becomes weak and we become complacent and discouraged, we are reluctant to pray.*

changes around us. You may never know who is experiencing depression, heartbreak, or domestic violence, but if you pray, your prayers can cause people to get a breakthrough.

Personal Testimony

This topic was actully inspired by my spiritual dad, whom I love so much. Here I am writing a book about prayer and he is teaching and preaching to us about how we need to seek God for the prayer mantle. I'm in awe of God, and I believe with all my heart that God not only confirms what he has given to me but also helps me not doubt what he puts in my heart. Whatever God has shown you through visions or dreams, do not doubt it because doubt will cancel out his divine assignment for you. Always remember to seek God in all you do and follow his direction because he will never lead you down the wrong path. He is too wise to make a mistake and too powerful for his plan not to come together. Believe what God says not only to you but about you. His track record is good. Everything in the Bible came to pass, is about to happen, or will happen later. Don't let the enemy fool you. God is a God of opportunity, and opportunity does not knock only once. God is a God of chances; don't quit when you are about to cross the finish line into your destiny. If you are experiencing tribulations, it's an indication that you are in a state of birthing the promises of God into your life.

Prayer

Oh Lord, I pray that you will bless me indeed and enlarge my territory. Let me not cause anyone pain during this process. Help me to understand that you are with me even in my troubles. Thank you for hearing my prayer. Lord, I pray that you will give me a desire for prayer and help me to be concerned about the people around me, in Jesus's name.

Praying is having faith to believe that God hears us when we pray in Jesus's name.

Jesus Prays

> Very early in the morning, while it was still dark, Jesus got up, left the house, and went off to a solitary place, where he prayed. Simon and his companions went to look for him. (Mark 1:35–36 NIV)

If you ask a true believer about prayer, I guarantee one of his or her responses will be that prayer works. Prayer is the most important activity in the body of Christ, yet it is the least-exercised practice among the believers. Ironically, it was the highlight of Jesus's ministry. Jesus expects us to do greater works on the earth through his name, but we cannot fulfill that assignment until we pick up a burden for prayer. Jesus is not asking us to do something that has not been done before; he just wants us to follow his example. Jesus recorded the model for prayer, and he often prayed himself. When we read the synoptic gospels, we will find many occasions when Jesus prayed via a Jewish background. He followed the Jewish tradition by often visiting the temple. Luke 4:15-20 (NIV) says,

> He was teaching in their synagogues, and everyone praised him. He went to Nazareth, where he had been brought up, and on the Sabbath day, he went into the synagogue, as was his custom. He stood up to read, and the scroll of the prophet Isaiah was

> handed to him. Unrolling it, he found the place where it is written: "The Spirit of the LORD is on me because he has anointed me to proclaim good news to the poor. He has sent me to proclaim freedom for the prisoners and recovery of sight for the blind, to set the oppressed free, to proclaim the year of the LORD's favor." Then he rolled up the scroll, gave it back to the attendant and sat down. The eyes of everyone in the synagogue were fastened on him.

There is no doubt in my mind that Jesus prayed before he read the scripture on that day.

Jesus prayed for guidance and directions before he chose his disciples. "One of those days, Jesus went out to a mountainside to pray and spent the night praying to God. When morning came, he called his disciples to him and chose twelve of them, whom he also designated apostles" (Luke 6:12–13 NIV). "Simon, Simon, Satan has asked to sift all of you as wheat. But I have prayed for you, Simon, that your faith may not fail. And when you have turned back, strengthen your brothers" (Luke 22:31–32 NIV). Jesus intercedes for Peter when the enemy requested him. I am a firm believer that the enemy knew that Peter had potential and he wanted to boycott Peter's assignment. Jesus prays for Peter so he could be strengthened and encourage. Let us follow the example of Jesus and to remember to pray for our brothers and sister when their faith has been tested.

> Jesus went out as usual to the Mount of Olives, and his disciples followed him. On reaching the place, he said to them, "Pray that you will not fall into temptation." He withdrew about a stone's throw

beyond them, knelt down, and prayed. (Luke 22:39–41 NIV)

I believe that the body of Christ should seek the face of God more earnestly, especially when there is unction from the Holy Ghost. We should not fall so easily into temptation because prayer is our shield of defense. Jesus prays for our protection, so we must continue to pray for our own and others' protection.

My prayer is not that you take them out of the world but that you protect them from the evil one. They are not of the world, even as I am not of it. Sanctify them by the truth; your word is truth. As you sent me into the world, I have sent them into the world. For them, I sanctify myself, that they too may be truly sanctified. My prayer is not for them alone. I also pray for those who will believe in me through their message, that all of them may be one, Father, just as you are to me and I am in you. May they also be in us so that the world may believe that you have sent me. I have given them the glory that you gave me, that they may be one as we are one. (John 17:17–26 NIV)

Personal Testimony

I have had some excellent time in prayer with the Lord, and I can't stress enough that God will meet you if you want a better prayer life. Prayer is ongoing fellowship, so while I am at my job, I can pray. While I'm traveling, whether on public transportation or in my car, I can pray. While I am worshiping at the house of God and I see something that is out of order, I should pray instead of complaining and sowing seeds of discord among the brethren. I have learned so much from writing this book, and my prayer is that I will strive to have a better prayer life.

Prayer

Father, I pray that each person who is reading this right now will increase his or her prayers in life. Help the person to make the necessary changes to have a closer walk with you. Father, I pray we will take heed of the spirit when you are calling us to a higher place, knowing that prayer will take us further in our relationship with you. Lord, increase my love for prayer, and give me the will to pray. In Jesus's name, amen.

Prayer Targets

> Therefore I exhort first of all that supplications, prayers, intercessions, and giving of thanks be made for all men, for kings and all who are in authority, that we may lead a quiet and peaceable life in all godliness and reverence. For this is good and acceptable in the sight of God our Savior. (1 Timothy 1:2–3 KJV)

The apostle Paul gave Timothy a charge. He wanted to make sure that prayer, intercession, and thanksgiving were made for all people. We cannot be prejudiced in our prayers and only pray for those in our inner circles. Jesus had twelve disciples, and from that twelve he had an inner circle of three, but he did not discriminate. He was available to all people. In fact, he made the statement that his "house should be called a house of prayer" (Luke 19:46). Likewise, we cannot be biased about who comes into our worship center and needs prayers. We may have different skin

> *we cannot be biased about who comes into our worship center and needs prayers.*

colors and come from different backgrounds, but all of us need prayer.

We are to pray for the sinners who need salvation. Pray for your unsaved loved one that he or she will accept Jesus Christ as his or her savior. Pray for those who are incarcerated because they may be locked up, but they are not locked out from the presence of God. Pray for your families, that God would cause harmony in your home. Pray for your coworkers, that God would draw their attention to himself and save them. Pray for the people you ride the bus/train with while you are going to work. Pray that God will touch their hearts and that they will have an encounter with the Lord Jesus Christ.

Pray for the homeless, that God will provide shelter. Pray for the orphans, that they find placement in homes that have a moral standard and godly influences. Pray for your enemies, that God will bless them. Pray for your neighbors, that God will bring drastic changes in the neighborhood where you reside. Pray for believers, that they will be steadfast in adversity. Pray for godly marriages and rebuke the spirit of divorce. Pray for your pastor, that God will keep his or her feet from slipping and give him or her strength to preach the word of God without compromise. Pray for governors and presidents so they will make moral laws. Pray for the peace of Jerusalem. Pray for believers so we can become one as Jesus prayed. *Pray for laborers so the church of God can grow.*

Prayer has no boundaries, and there is no distance in prayer. That means I can live in the United States of America and send a prayer to Africa, the Caribbean, or any part in the world. Wherever you reside, you can pray for another city, state, or country. God is relying on us to stand in the gap. Will you accept the challenge to pray for those in need? Remember, prayer is not an option. For us it must be something we live by. God does not renege on his word. He expects the command to be carried out. And he will use anyone who is available and willing to be in partnership with him to carry out his plan on the earth. Will you be the one? We cannot give up on praying because our prayers may not manifest yet. We have to remind ourselves that prayer is a discipline and a practice of our Christian belief. We must wait patiently on God, knowing that he will answer. God has given us the power of the Holy Ghost, who will assist us in prayer, so we do not have to be afraid to pray. Just start talking to God and develop a habit of prayer. Ask the Lord to help you to have compassion and to be able to discern the needs of the people around you so you can travail for them in prayer. Instead of us criticizing, we should accept the challenge to pray. Be committed and consistent on a regular basis to pray, and seal every prayer in Jesus's name.

Different Prayer Postures

- **Kneeling/bowing:** Psalm 95:6 (KJV)

  Come, let us worship and bow down, Let us kneel before the LORD our Maker.

- **Sitting**: 2 Samuel 7:18 (KJV)

  Then went king David in, and sat before the LORD, and he said, Who am I, O Lord GOD? and what is my house, that thou hast brought me hitherto?

- **Standing**: Job 30:20 (NIV)

  I cry out to you, God, but you do not answer; I stand up, but you merely look at me.

- **Walking:** 2Kings 4:35 (NIV)

  Elisha turned away and walked back and forth in the room and then got on the bed stretched out on him once more. The boy sneezed seven times and opened his eyes.

➤ **Lying down:** Deuteronomy 9:25 (KJV)

Thus I fell down before the LORD forty days and forty nights, as I fell down *at the first*; because the LORD had said he would destroy you.

Balancing the equation

Sin - _____ = God's judgment

Intercession (Genesis 18:20–21).

My people + _____ = Heal their land

humble themselves, pray, seek my face (2 Chronicles 7:14).

Praying + _____ = spare the people

Giving ownership back on God (Exodus 32:12).

Believed in the Lord + Believed in his prophets = _____
caused you to Prosper (2 Chronicles 20:20).

Prayer + Fasting = _____ casting out demon (Matthew 7:21).

This is the confidence that we have in him that + if we ask any thing according his will he = _____ he hears us (1 John 5:14).

Scripture References

Chapter 1

Luke 18:1 KJV
Jer. 29:12 NIV
Heb. 4:15-16 NKJV
Jer. 33:3 KJV
Gen. 1:26 KJV
Gen. 2:19-20
Gen. 2:4-3:24 KJV
Rom. 11:29 KJV
Phil. 4:6 NKJ
Lev. 25:25 KJV
2 Kings 4:1 KJV
Acts 6 KJV
Luke 1:37 KJV
Rom. 3:23 KJV
2 Cor. 5:17 NLT
Eph. 2:8 NIV
Luke 23:34 KJV
Heb. 9:22 KJV
Matt. 7:1-3 MSG
1 Chron. 4:10 HCSB

Gal. 6:3-4 NIV
Heb. 12:1 NLT
Num. 20:11 – 12 NIV
1Tim 3:5 NIV
John 11:44 KJV
Luke 11:1 NKJ
Matt. 6:6 KJV
Matt. 6:11 KJV
John 14:13-14 KJV
Gen 22 KJV
Jude 1:20 KJV
Ps. 34:8 KJV
Ps. 4:1 KJV
Ps. 5:3 NLT
Exod. 3:7 – 10 KJV
Exod. 25:22 KJV
1 Sam. 3 KJV
John 10:27 KJV
2 Chron 7:14 NKJV

Chapter 2

1 Sam. 1:12-15 KJV
1 Sam. 2: 1KJV
Gen. 24:42- 49 KJV
Prov. 3:5-6 KJV
1 King 22:1-53 KJV
John 11 KJV
Ps. 66:18 The Word in Life Study Bible
Ps. 51 NIV
Phil. 2:7 NLT
Gen. 3 KJV
Gen. 12:1-2 KJV
Gen. 16:1 – 4 NLT
Gen. 30 KJV

Ps. 24:14 KJV
Lam. 3:25 KJV
Isa. 30:18 KJV
Micah 7:7 KJV
1 John 5:14- 15 NLT
Acts 1:3-5 KJV
Hab. 2:2-4 TLB
1 kings 8:44-54
Job 1:6-8 KJV
Dan. 6:10 KJV
Dan. 6:20 KJV
Ps. 34:19 KJV
John 16:33

Chapter 3

Matt. 7:7 KJV
John 15:7 KJV
Rom. 10:14 KJV
Gen. 11 KJV
Isa. 65:24 NLT
Acts 12:1-9 KJV
John 14:27 KJV
Amos 3:3 NIV
Job 22:28 KJV
Acts 27 KJV
Acts 3 KJV
Luke 5:4-8 KJV
Josh. 6:1-13 KJV
Num. 23:19 NLT
Joel 1:14 KJV

Matt. 56:16-18 NIV
Mark 8:34 KJV
Luke 4:2 KJV
Ezra 10 KJV
Esth. 4:16KJV
Acts 9:9 KJV
Dan. 10:3 KJV
2 Peter 3:5 KJV
Matt. 17:21 KJV
Isa. 58:3 KJV
2 Chron. 20:1-4NKJV
2 Chron. 20:14-17 NKJV
Esth. 4:16 KJV
Matt.4:4 KJV

Chapter 4

Ezek. 22:30 KJV
Isa. 59:16 KJV
2 Cor. 10:4-5 KJV
Matt. 11:25 KJV
Ps. 24:3-4 KJV
Luke 11:38 KJV
Exod. 30:17-21 KJV
Exod. 40:30-32 KJV
1 Tim. 2:8 NLT
Ps. 26: 2 KJV
Gen. 18:23-24 NKJV
Jas. 1:6-8 KJV

Rom. 8:26 KJV
1 John 4:20 KJV
Acts 17:28 KJV
1 Peter 4:8 NLT
Mark 2:2-11 NIV
Gal 6:2 KJV
Luke 7:2 -10 NIV
Matt 6:34 NIV
Exod. 32:1-2 TLB
Exod. 7-14 TLB
Matt. 4 KJV

Chapter 5

John 4:23-24 KJV
Matt. 26:6-13 KJV
John 1:14 KJV
Rom 12:1 KJV

John 9:31 KJV
Ps. 8:4-6 KJV
Isa. 14:13 NIV
Rev. 12:8-9 KJV

Chapter 6

Isa. 62:6 NIV
Matt. 6:10 KJV
Heb. 13:8 KJV
Luke 15:11-32 KJV
Isa. 1:19 NIV
Ps. 8:1-13 NIV
John 1:9 KJV
Ps. 107:1 NIV
1 Thess. 5:18 NIV
Jas. 4:3 NIV
Eph. 6:18

Matt. 18:1920 NIV
Prov. 27:17 NIV
Acts 16:26 NIV
Mark 1:35-36 NIV
Luke 4:15-20 NIV
Luke 6:12- 13 NIV
Luke 22:31-32 NIV
Luke 22:39-41 NIV
John 17:17-26 NIV
1 Tim 1:2-3 KJV
Luke 19:46 KJV

Endnotes

1 www.timeanddate.com (Accessed November 2017)

1997. In *Holman Concise Bible Dictionary,* by Broadman & Holman Reference, 236. Nasville: B&H Publishing Group.

1988. In *Growing towards Spiritual Maturity,* 47. Wheaton: Evangelical Training Association.